SMALL HOUSES
PETITES MAISONS
KLEINE HÄUSER

SMALL HOUSES
PETITES MAISONS
KLEINE HÄUSER

EVERGREEN

EVERGREEN is an imprint of

Taschen GmbH

© 2006 TASCHEN GmbH

Hohenzollernring 53, D-50672 Köln

www.taschen.com

Editor Editrice Redakteur:
Simone Schleifer

English proof reading Relecture anglaise Korrektur lesen:
Matthew Clarke

French translation Traduction française Französische Übersetzung:
Marion Westerhoff

German translation Traduction allemande Deutsche Übersetzung:
Grusche Rosenkranz

Art director Direction artistique Art Direktor:
Mireia Casanovas Soley

Graphic design and layout Mise en page et maquette Graphische Gestaltung und Layout:
Diego González

Printed by Imprimé en Gedruckt durch:
Artes Gráficas Toledo, S.A.U., Spain

ISBN: 3-8228-4176-5

The small house has been a recurring theme in architecture, whether as an academic exercise or as a spontaneous vernacular response to man's basic need for shelter. Examples range from Native American tents to the Kolonihaven contemporary architecture park in Denmark, which has served as a theoretical framework for esthetic thought on small homes. The design of a minimal house has to tackle a wide range of problems, and adapt both form and function to the structural system and technical definitions. The resolution of these problems in a building of small proportions can result in highly precise and efficient structures.

The basic functions of the house have to be established to simplify the task as much as possible. In order to optimize the usable space, it is often necessary to resort to mechanisms or components that serve two or more functions at the same time. From a formal standpoint, the minimal house must be based on a very rational plan. Pure shapes, generally orthogonal, adapt best, and inside, divisions created by walls are avoided as much as possible, in favor of open, continuous spaces containing most of the functions. Due to their proportions—often related to the budget—minimal houses tend to use a basic, light structural system, generally based on wooden frames or thin metal sections, which also make the building easy to construct on isolated or inaccessible plots of land. These homes can hide ingenious elements inside, such as folding tables, hanging beds, translucent panels, and highly efficient storage areas.

Just as modern machines have microchips that hold vast amounts of data, architects now have very thin materials to replace others that took up a great deal more space. There include thin metal sections that serve as structural systems; plywood systems that provide the final finish for surfaces; and very dense but extremely fine materials that provide thermal and acoustic insulation. This means that the modern architect can cater to today's requirements by producing a high-quality, efficient structure with the help of the latest technology. This is reflected in spaces that do not sacrifice one iota of their abundant creativity and sophisticated design to their minimal size.

This collection of 25 projects includes practical, contemporary examples that demonstrate the countless architectural solutions available for houses with minimal space.

Le concept de petite maison est un thème architectural récurrent, sous forme d'exercice académique ou de réponse vernaculaire au besoin humain primordial de s'abriter. L'éventail des exemples s'étend des tentes des natifs américains au parc d'architecture contemporaine de Kolonihaven au Danemark, utilisé comme cadre théorique dans la conception esthétique de petites habitations. Le design d'une maison minimaliste doit résoudre toute une série de problèmes, dans un souci d'harmoniser la fonction et la forme aux structures et aux définitions techniques. La résolution de ces problèmes dans une construction aux proportions minimales peut aboutir à des structures extrêmement précises et efficaces.

Les fonctions essentielles de la maison doivent viser à simplifier la tâche au maximum. Pour optimaliser l'espace utilisable, il faut souvent avoir recours à des mécanismes ou à des éléments aux fonctions polyvalentes. Sur le plan formel, la maison minimaliste repose sur un concept très rationnel. Les formes épurées, généralement orthogonales sont idéales. A l'intérieur, on élimine les murs, autant que possible, pour favoriser les espaces continus polyvalents. De par leurs dimensions −souvent liées au budget− les maisons minimalistes utilisent en général un système simple, de structure légère souvent constituée de châssis en bois ou de fines cloisons de métal, facilitant la construction de la maison sur des terrains isolés ou inaccessibles. Ces maisons cachent souvent des systèmes ingénieux, sous forme de tables pliantes, lits-mezzanine, cloisons translucides et zones de rangement astucieuses.

A l'instar même des machines modernes munies de micro puces stockant un grand nombre de données, les architectes disposent de nos jours de matériaux extrêmement minces, se substituant à leurs prédécesseurs plus volumineux : éléments en matériaux légers servant de structures, formes en contreplaqué pour parachever les surfaces, matériaux compacts mais légers pour l'isolation thermique et acoustique. De nos jours, grâce à la technologie de pointe la plus récente, l'architecte moderne peut réaliser un produit de grande qualité, répondant aux critères et exigences actuels. Ceci se reflète dans ces espaces qui ne sacrifient pas un iota de leur richesse créative ou de leur design sublime sur l'autel du minimalisme.

Cette collection, riche de 25 projets, est un éventail d'exemples pratiques, contemporains, proposant d'innombrables solutions architecturales permettant de créer des maisons dans un espace minimal.

Das kleine Haus ist ein immer wiederkehrendes Thema in der Architektur, sei es als akademische Übung oder als spontane Antwort auf die Bedürfnisse des Menschen nach einer Unterkunft. Beispiele reichen von den Zelten der amerikanischen Ureinwohner zu dem zeitgenössischen Architekturpark Kolonihaven in Dänemark, der den theoretischen Rahmen für die Ästhetik kleiner Behausungen bietet. Beim Entwurf eines Minimalhauses müssen eine Reihe von Voraussetzungen berücksichtigt werden. Form und Funktion müssen gleichzeitig an die Struktur und die technischen Vorgaben angepasst werden. Die Auflösung dieser Probleme in Form von Gebäuden kleiner Proportionen kann zu Bauten mit präzisen und effizienten Strukturen führen.

Damit diese Aufgabe so weit wie möglich vereinfacht werden kann, müssen die Grundfunktionen der Häuser festgelegt werden. Um die Nutzfläche der Häuser zu maximieren, muss oft auf Mechanismen oder Komponenten zurückgegriffen werden, die gleichzeitig mehreren Zwecken dienen. Vom formalen Standpunkt aus gesehen, muss ein Minimalhaus auf einem sehr rationalen Plan basieren. Klare Formen, in der Regel rechtwinklig, sind dafür am besten geeignet. Inneneinteilungen durch Wände werden zu weit wie möglich vermieden, statt dessen werden offene, durchgehende Räume bevorzugt, die mehrere Funktionen auf einmal vereinen. Aufgrund der kleinen Proportionen, die oft auf ein begrenztes Budget zurückzuführen sind, werden beim Bau von Minimalhäusern leichte Strukturen verwendet. In der Regel sind dies Konstruktionen aus Holz oder dünnen Metallprofilen, die den Bau auch auf abgelegenem oder unzugänglichem Gelände möglich machen. Diese Häuser enthalten im Inneren oft ausgefeilte Elemente zur optimalen Platzausnutzung, wie beispielsweise originelle Klapptische, Hängebetten, durchsichtige Paneele und effizienten Stauraum.

So wie moderne Maschinen mit Mikrochips ausgerüstet sind, die eine umfassende Menge an Daten enthalten, haben Architekten heutzutage besonders dünne Materialien zur Verfügung, die an Stelle der früher verwendeten Stoffe treten, die wesentlich mehr Platz in Anspruch nahmen. Dazu gehören dünne Metallprofile, die als Struktur dienen, Sperrholzkonstruktionen für die Oberflächenverarbeitung und extrem dünne Materialien mit hoher Dichte, die für optimale Wärme- und Schallisolierung sorgen. Dies bedeutet, dass der Architekt von heute auf die aktuellen Anforderungen reagieren und unter Einsatz modernster Technologien hochwertige und effektive Lösungen anbieten kann. Dies zeigt sich auch an den hier vorgestellten Beispielen, bei denen die geringe Größe Kreativität und ausgefeiltem Design in keiner Weise entgegensteht.

Diese Kollektion von insgesamt 25 Projekten enthält aktuelle, praktische Beispiele gelungener Lösungen für Minimalhäuser.

SMALL HOUSES
PETITES MAISONS
KLEINE HÄUSER

Wenger House
Maison Wenger
Wenger Haus

Heidi and Peter Wenger

Situated at an altitude of 6,500 feet in the Swiss Alps, this tiny vacation home was designed as a place to spend short periods in the mountains. The framework, a simple system of sloping beams, marks the interior space and has the same shape as the roofs of the region's traditional houses. The primary material, wood, is used for both the structural elements and the interior finishings and the basic layout consists of two floors and a single space. The lower level contains the living room, dining room, and kitchen, while the upper, attic-style level, joined to the lower level by a spiral staircase, consists of the bedroom. When the house is occupied, the western façade, which is also a wooden platform, opens completely to create a balcony that extends the kitchen cabinets and the triangular doors in the outer wall, making the space truly multifunctional. Special care was taken with all the components to create a small-scale mechanical object that functions with great precision.

Située à une altitude de 2.000 m dans les Alpes suisses, cette maison minuscule a été conçue comme un endroit pour courts séjours en montagne. La structure, un système simple de poutres inclinées qui définit l'espace intérieur, épouse la forme de la toiture des maisons traditionnelles de la région. La matière première, le bois, est utilisée à la fois pour les éléments de la structure et pour les finitions intérieures. Le plan de base comprend deux étages et un seul espace. Le niveau inférieur héberge le salon, la salle à manger et la cuisine. Le niveau supérieur, style mansarde, relié à l'étage inférieur par un escalier en colimaçon, abrite la chambre à coucher. Quant la maison est habitée, la façade ouest, qui est aussi une plate-forme de bois, s'ouvre complètement pour former un balcon qui agrandit la cuisine et les portes triangulaires dans le mur extérieur, créant un espace véritablement polyvalent. Tous les éléments ont été étudiés avec le plus grand soin pour créer un mécanisme à petite échelle qui fonctionne avec une précision d'horloger.

Dieses kleine Wochenendhaus wurde auf einer Höhe von 2.000 m in den Schweizer Alpen erbaut und soll hauptsächlich als Feriendomizil oder Wochenendhaus in den Bergen dienen. Das Rahmenwerk, ein einfaches System schräger Balken, bestimmt den Innenraum und weist dieselbe Form auf wie die Dächer der traditionellen Häuser dieser Gegend. Als vorrangiges Baumaterial wurde Holz gewählt. Das Haus besteht aus zwei Stockwerken und einem einzigen Raum. Im unteren Bereich liegen Wohnzimmer, Esszimmer und die Küche, während im oberen Dachbereich, der mit dem unteren durch eine Wendeltreppe verbunden ist, das Schlafzimmer untergebracht wurde. Die westliche Fassade, ebenfalls eine hölzerne Plattform, kann ganz geöffnet werden um einen Balkon zu bilden, der die Küchenschränke und die dreieckigen Türen in der Außenwand optisch verlängert. Besondere Aufmerksamkeit wurde auf die einzelnen Bauelemente gelegt, um ein kleines, mechanisches Objekt in bewährter schweizerischer Präzision zu schaffen.

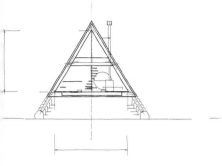

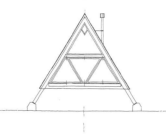

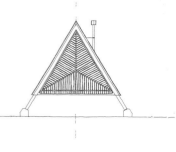

ɔss section Section transversale Querschnitt

Elevations Élévations Aufrisse

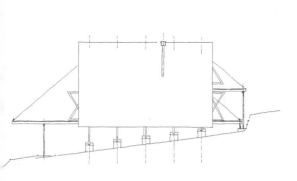

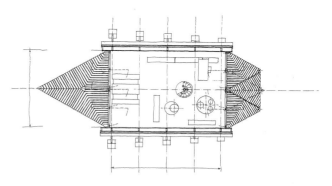

vation Élévation Aufriss

Ground floor Rez-de-chaussée Erdgeschoss

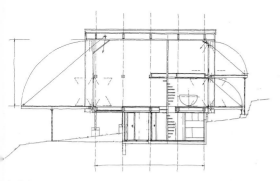

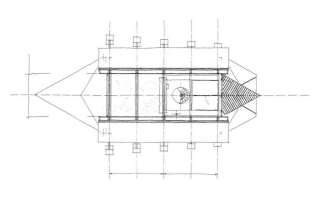

gitudinal section Section longitudinale Längsschnitt

First floor Premier étage Erstes Obergeschoss

To make the most of the minimal interior space, elements such as the kitchen unit can be opened and closed.

Pour optimiser l'intérieur minimaliste, certains éléments, à l'instar du bloc cuisine peuvent être ouverts ou fermés.

Um den geringen Raum im Inneren optimal auszunutzen, können Elemente wie die Küchenecke geöffnet und geschlossen werden.

The basic shape of the house's design and the use of wood as the primary material reflect traditional Alpine architecture.

Le concept de base du design de la maison et l'emploi du bois, reflètent l'architecture alpine traditionnelle.

Die Grundform des Hauses und die Verwendung von Holz als Hauptbaustoff spiegeln die traditionelle Bauweise der Alpen wieder.

The fold-out balcony on the western façade and the triangular pivoting windows create a rich composition of juxtaposed planes.

balcon pliable sur la façade ouest et les fenêtres triangulaires pivotantes créent une intéressante composition de plans juxtaposés.

r Balkon an der Westseite und die Erkerfenster bilden eine abwechslungsreiche Komposition an Fassadenelementen.

Stein-Fleischmann House
Maison Stein-Fleischmann
Stein-Fleischmann Haus

Jacques Moussafir/Moussafir Architectes Associés

This small house situated near Paris was built by the internationally renowned architect Jacques Moussafir for a young couple and their two children. The residence consists of two parts: a cube-shape pavilion that runs parallel to the street and a wing that connects it to the front building. The colorful ground floor is defined by the limits of the garden, while the whole house is crossed by an axis of light leading to the exterior. On the upper level, a large, white space flooded with light is governed by a strict geometry. Seven large picture windows provide fragmented views, disrupted by the oblique, vertical views of the neighboring buildings' silhouettes. The architect compared the views from the house with the effect of looking through a kaleidoscope, which transforms the banal surroundings into a collage of transfigured reality.

Cette petite maison située prés de Paris a été construite par l'architecte Jacques Moussafir, de renommée internationale, pour un jeune couple et ses trois enfants. La résidence présente deux parties : un pavillon en forme de cube, parallèle à la rue et une aile qui le relie à l'édifice principal. Le rez-de-chaussée, très coloré, se prolonge au ras du jardin et l'ensemble de la maison est traversé par un axe de lumière dirigé vers l'extérieur. A l'étage supérieur, un vaste espace, inondé de lumière, est placé sous le signe d'une géométrie des plus strictes. Sept fenêtres larges, à l'instar de tableaux, créent des vues fragmentées, interrompues par les vues obliques et verticales des silhouettes des bâtiments environnants. L'architecte a comparé les vues depuis la maison, à l'effet produit par un kaléidoscope, transformant la banalité des environs en un collage surréaliste.

Dieses kleine Haus in der Nähe von Paris wurde von dem international bekannten Architekten Jacques Moussafir für ein junges Paar und deren zwei Kinder entworfen. Das Haus besteht aus zwei Teilen: ein kubusförmiger Pavillon parallel zur Straße und einen Flügel, der mit dem Vordergebäude verbunden ist. Das farbenfrohe Erdgeschoss wird durch die Grenzlinien des Gartens definiert, während das gesamte Haus von einer Lichtachse durchsetzt ist, die nach außen weist. Auf der oberen Etage wird ein großer, weißer und mit Licht durchfluteter Bereich von einer strikten Geometrie bestimmt. Sieben große Fenster bieten fragmentartige Ausblicke, die durch die indirekten vertikalen Aussichten auf die Silhouetten der Nachbargebäude unterbrochen werden. Der Architekt hat die Ausblicke aus dem Haus mit dem Effekt eines Kaleidoskops verglichen, das die banale Umgebung in eine Kollage verformter Realität verwandelt.

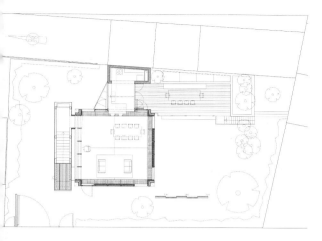

Plan Plan Grundriss

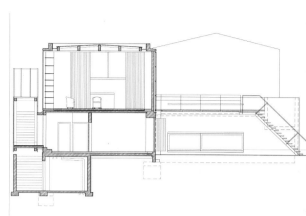

Section Section Schnitt

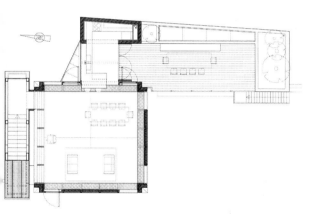

First floor Premier étage Erstes Obergeschoss

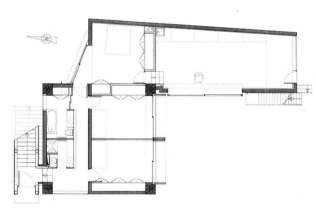

Ground floor Rez-de-chaussée Erdgeschoss

The house is made up of two parts: a cube-shape pavilion that runs parallel to the street and a wing that connects it to the front building.

La maison est en deux parties : un pavillon en forme de cube, parallèle à la rue et une aile qui lui est relié.

Das Haus besteht aus einem Pavillon in Würfelform parallel zur Straße und einem Flügel, der es mit dem Vordergebäude verbindet.

A translucent partition wall serves as a enormous bookshelf and storage space, while allowing natural light to flow in from the exterior.
Une cloison translucidè fait office d'immense bibliothèque et d'espace de rangement, tout en laissant passer la lumière naturelle vers l'intérieur.
Eine durchscheinende Zwischenwand dient als Bücherregal und Stauraum und lässt Licht hinein.

Dodds House
Maison Dodds
Dodds Haus

Engelen Moore

This small house is located in the suburbs of Sydney, in a mixed neighborhood of residential complexes and industrial buildings. All of the house's dimensions are determined by the standard measurements of the panels covering its entire surface. The unified, solid appearance was reinforced by painting all the exterior elements the same silver color, thus giving all the materials the same finish. Inside, the layout is almost completely open-plan. A two-story living room—which includes a small loft for sleeping—provides a sense of transparency and spaciousness. The space extends even further, through the sliding glass doors that open onto an interior patio on the north side. Other doors, at right angles to the sliding doors, open to the east, where a long pool separates the house from the preexisting party wall, with its original brickwork exposed to view. The two levels are connected by sheet-metal stairs supported by a continuous yellow block.

Cette petite maison est située dans la banlieue de Sydney, dans un voisinage où se mêlent complexes résidentiels et bâtiments industriels. Toutes les dimensions de la maison découlent des mesures standards des panneaux qui en recouvrent toute la superficie. Cette apparence d'unité compacte est renforcée par le revêtement argent peint sur tous les extérieurs, conférant ainsi à tous les matériaux le même fini. A l'intérieur, le volume est presque entièrement ouvert. Le salon sur deux étages –intégrant un petit loft pour dormir– dégage une sensation de transparence et d'espace, accentuée par des portes en verre coulissantes qui s'ouvrent au nord sur un patio intérieur. D'autres portes, placées à angle droit des portes coulissantes, s'ouvrent vers l'est où une piscine tout en longueur sépare la maison de la cloison préexistante, rehaussant sa maçonnerie de briques. Un escalier en lattes de métal, soutenu par un seul bloc jaune, relie les deux niveaux entre eux.

Dieses kleine Haus liegt in einem Vorort von Sydney. Sämtliche Dimensionen des Hauses werden von den Standardabmessungen der Paneele begrenzt, mit denen das gesamte Haus bedeckt wurde. Dieses vereinheitlichte, solide Aussehen des Hauses wurde noch durch einen silberfarbenen Anstrich einzelner Elemente des Gebäudes verstärkt. Innen wirkt das Haus eher groß und offen. Ein zweistöckiger Wohnraum mit einer abgetrennten kleineren Schlafebene vermittelt einen Eindruck von Transparenz und Weite. Dieses Gefühl von Geräumigkeit wird noch durch die Glasschiebetüren verstärkt, die in einen Innenhof an der Nordseite führen. Weitere Türen, die im rechten Winkel zu den Schiebetüren angebracht sind, weisen nach Osten, wo ein langer Pool das Haus von der bestehenden Seitenmauer trennt, deren ursprüngliche Ziegelsteine freigelegt wurden. Die beiden Ebenen sind durch Treppen aus Walzblech miteinander verbunden, die durch einen durchgängigen gelben Steinblock gestützt werden.

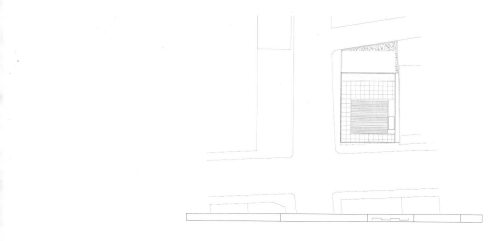

Plan Plan Grundriss

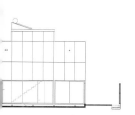

...ngitudinal sections Sections longitudinales Längsschnitte

Plans Plans Grundrisse

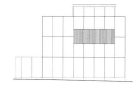

...vations Élévations Aufrisse

Sections Sections Schnitte

Thin aluminum panels cover the building's entire outer surface, giving the house an industrial image that manages to reflect subtle refinement.

De minces panneaux d'aluminium habillent toute la surface extérieure de l'édifice, lui conférant des allures de bâtiment industriel, doté d'une subtile élégance.

Dünne Aluminiumtafeln bedecken die gesamte Außenfläche des Gebäudes und verleihen dem Haus das Aussehen eines Industriegebäudes.

The house has natural cross-ventilation, thanks to the large sliding windows and adjustable glass blinds.

La maison bénéficie d'une ventilation croisée grâce à de grandes baies vitrées coulissantes et à des persiennes modulables.

Die großen Schiebefenster und beweglichen Glasblenden sorgen für eine perfekte Ventilation.

☐ City Cube

Oishi Kazuhiku Architect Atelier

City Cube is designed as a standard model for a three-story, urban residence with a concise structural system intended to reduce construction costs. The layout is a 30-foot square that is divided into small individual grids, enabling the nine spaces to be divided into segments. The private areas, including the bedroom, bathroom, and guest room, were allocated to the first floor. An office space was also created to allow the occupant to work from home. In the center, a tube of light penetrates the three levels, which have a spiral stairway built into them. The verticality of the staircase attempts to represent the transience of natural light produced by the movement of the sun and clouds through a translucent glass box, creating a sensitive abstraction of natural phenomena. Using a cubic space within the urban environment, the building focuses on providing its occupants with comfort living while retaining a close relationship with the city and the surrounding natural environment.

Le City Cube est un module standard pour une résidence urbaine de trois étages dotée d'une structure simple conçue pour réduire le coût de la construction. Le plan est un carré de 9 mètres divisé en petites grilles permettant de répartir les neuf espaces en segments. Les sphères privées, à savoir la chambre à coucher, la salle de bains et la chambre d'invités sont situées au premier étage. Un espace bureau a été conçu pour que l'occupant puisse travailler chez lui. Au centre, un tube de lumière traverse les trois niveaux, auxquels un escalier hélicoïdal est intégré. La verticalité de l'escalier tente de représenter le caractère éphémère de la lumière naturelle issue du déplacement du soleil et des nuages au travers d'une boîte translucide, créant ainsi la sensation abstraite du phénomène naturel. A l'instar d'un cube plongé dans l'environnement urbain, le bâtiment doit offrir à ses occupants un espace de vie confortable tout en gardant un lien étroit avec la ville et l'environnement naturel des alentours.

City Cube wurde als standardisiertes Modell für eine dreigeschossige Stadtwohnung konzipiert, mit deren übersichtliches System die Baukosten merklich reduziert werden sollen. Grundlage ist ein 9 m² großes Gebäude, das in kleine, voneinander unabhängige Raster unterteilt ist. Diese neun Flächen können wiederum in einzelne Segmente aufgeteilt werden. Die Privaträume, darunter Schlafzimmer, Badezimmer und Gästezimmer, wurden auf der ersten Etage untergebracht. Damit die Bewohner auch von Zuhause aus arbeiten können wurde ein Büroraum mit in die Struktur eingebunden. In der Mitte führt ein Lichthof durch die drei Ebenen, in den auch eine Wendeltreppe eingebaut ist. Durch die Verwendung eines kubistischen Elementes innerhalb des städtischen Umfelds konzentriert sich die Funktion des Gebäudes auf den Wohnkomfort während gleichzeitig eine enge Bindung mit der Stadt und der natürlichen Umgebung beibehalten wird.

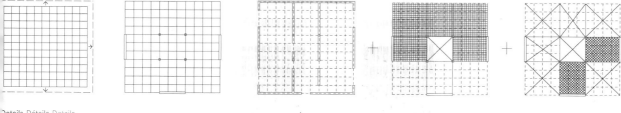

Details Détails Details

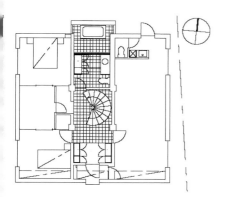 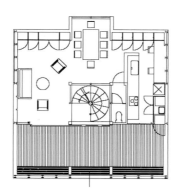 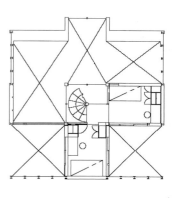

Ground floor Rez-de-chaussée Erdgeschoss

First floor Premier étage Erstes Obergeschoss

Second floor Deuxième étage Zweite Obergeschoss

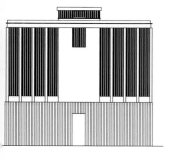 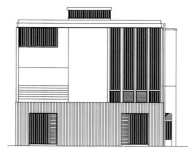

vations Élévations Aufrisse

Section Section Schnitt

This symmetrical structure, spread over three levels, was divided along the lines of a grid system in order to optimize space.

Cette structure symétrique, répartie sur trois niveaux, est divisée selon les lignes d'un système de grille afin d'optimiser l'espace.

Diese symmetrische Struktur geht über drei Etagen. Zur Platzoptimierung wurde sie entlang den Linien eines Gitters abgeteilt.

A wooden deck terrace is located along the south side of the second floor.

Une terrasse de bois longe le côté sud du deuxième étage.

Im zweiten Stock verläuft an der Südseite eine Terrasse mit Holzboden.

The layout revolves around a tube of light incorporating a spiral staircase that penetrates all three levels.

Le plan tourne autour d'un tube de lumière intégrant un escalier hélicoïdal qui traverse les trois étages.

Das Haus ist um ein Beleuchtungsrohr herum angelegt und enthält eine Wendeltreppe, die alle drei Etagen verbindet.

he private areas, including the bathroom, bedroom, and guest room, were allocated to the first floor.

les les sphères privées, à savoir, la salle de bains, la chambre à coucher et la chambre d'amis se situent au premier étage.

orivaten Räume wie Bad, Schlaf- und Gästezimmer liegen im ersten Stock.

☐ Tait-Doulgeris

Buzacott & Ocolisan associates

This project sought to remodel an old two-story house into a small family dwelling. The alterations took the form of large open spaces, including two bedrooms, a study and a north-facing swimming pool to the rear of the house. The width of the site allowed the architect considerable flexibility when it came to designing the service area, which lies on one of the sides, leaving room for open, light-flooded spaces. The ground floor is divided by a plywood structure that separates the living-dining room from the service facilities. When required, the threshold connecting the kitchen and the patio may be converted into an informal dining area. On the first floor, the same strategy of subdividing space was applied through the use of a wooden structure placed lengthwise in parallel to the stairs. The second-floor study opens onto a terrace with excellent views of the city and Harbor Bridge.

Ce projet tente de transformer une ancienne maison à deux étages en une demeure destinée à une petite famille. Ces modifications ont donné naissance à deux vastes espaces ouverts, comprenant deux chambres à coucher, un studio et une piscine face au Nord, derrière la maison. Grâce à la largeur du site, l'architecte a pu jouer d'une extraordinaire souplesse lors de la conception de la zone des services. Elle est située sur l'un des côtés, laissant le champ libre à des espaces inondés de lumière. Le rez-de-chaussée est divisé par une cloison en contreplaqué séparant le salon-salle à manger des installations domestiques. Le cas échéant, le palier reliant la cuisine au patio est modulable en un coin repas informel. Au premier étage, on retrouve le même principe de division de l'espace par le truchement d'une structure en bois longitudinale, parallèle aux escaliers. L'étude placée au deuxième étage s'ouvre sur une terrasse offrant une vue merveilleuse sur la ville et le Harbor Bridge.

Dieses Projekt sollte ein altes, zweigeschossiges Gebäude in ein kleineres Familienhaus umgebaut werden. Bei dem Umbau wurden große, offene Räume geschaffen, darunter zwei Schlafzimmer, ein Studio und ein nach Norden weisender Pool hinter dem Haus. Die Breite des Geländes hat dem Architekten eine gewisse Flexibilität bei der Gestaltung des Nutzbereiches erlaubt, der an einer der Seiten angelegt wurde. Das Erdgeschoss ist durch eine Sperrholzstruktur unterteilt, die den Wohn-/Essbereich vom Nutzbereich abtrennt. Falls erforderlich kann de Zwischenraum zwischen Küche und Innenhof in einen informellen Essbereich umgewandelt werden. Auf der ersten Etage wurde dieselbe Strategie der teilbaren Fläche eingesetzt und eine Holzstruktur parallel zum Treppenhaus errichtet. Das Studio auf der zweiten Etage weist auf eine Terrasse. Von hier aus genießt man einen herrlichen Blick auf die Stadt und die Harbor Bridge.

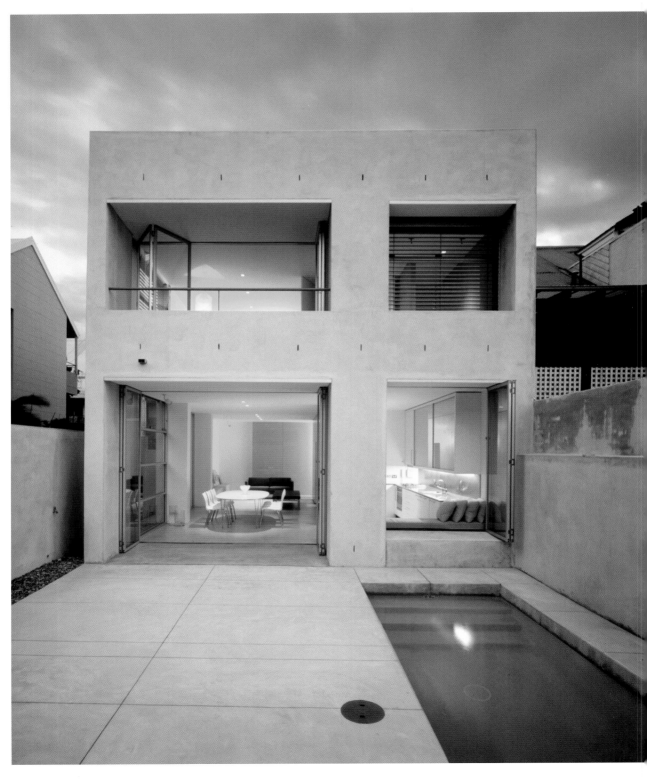

architecture is generally simple and makes use of few materials.

grand meuble de bois est placé dans le sens de la longueur, parallèlement à l'escalier pour diviser l'espace.

Architektur ist einfach und verwendet wenige Materialien.

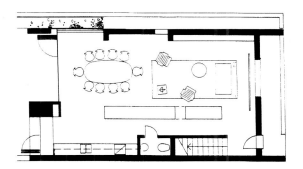

Ground floor Rez-de-chaussée Erdgeschoss

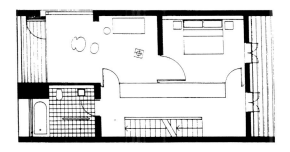

First floor Premier étage Erstes Obergeschoss

wooden furniture structure was placed lengthwise, parallel to the stairs, in order to divide the space.

ans l'ensemble, l'architecture est simple et met en scène peu de matériaux.

in Holzmöbel wurde als Raumteiler in Längsrichtung parallel zur Treppe platziert.

☐ Black Box

Andreas Henrikson

The architect's aim with this project was to come up with a structure that could be set up anywhere and was suitable for different purposes. Black Box is the name that was given to this project comprising a small, mobile, multifunctional home, because, according to its architect, it resembles a magician's box from the outside. The structure consists of a simple system of light, wooden frames that form a three-dimensional orthogonal weave covered by ninety, square chipboard panels. The panels' proportions and assembly mechanisms make constructing and dismantling the box an easy task. The roof is covered with a membrane of high-quality rubber that protects the house from water and climatic variables. The interior is a medium-sized two-story space. An open space on the upper level serves as a sleeping or work area. Below it are the services, kitchen, bathroom, and stairs, which are on one side of the cube.

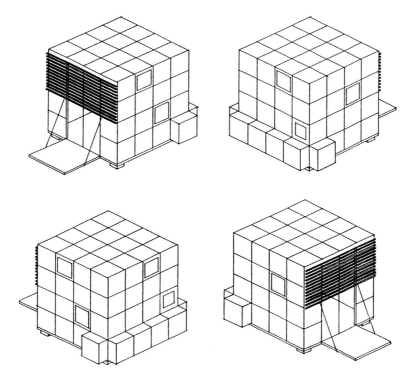

Dans ce projet, l'architecte a mis au point une structure poly-valente à même d'être installée partout. Ce projet est appelé Black Box −petite maison mobile, à fonctions multiples− par son architecte, car vu de l'extérieur, elle ressemble à une boîte de magicien. La structure comprend un système d'éclairage simple, une ossature en bois formant un volume orthogonal tri-dimensionnel, habillé de quatre-vingt dix panneaux carrés d'ag-gloméré. Les dimensions des panneaux et les mécanismes d'assemblage facilitent le montage et démontage de la boîte. Le toit est recouvert d'une membrane de caoutchouc de pre-mière qualité isolant la maison de l'eau et des variations climati-ques. L'espace intérieur, de taille moyenne, est réparti sur deux étages. A l'étage supérieur, l'espace ouvert sert à la fois de chambre ou de bureau. L'espace inférieur est réservé aux services : cuisine, salle de bains et escaliers situés sur un côté du cube.

Ziel des Architekten war es, eine Struktur zu entwickeln, die an jedem beliebigen Ort aufgebaut werden und dabei verschiede-nen Anforderungen genügen könnte. Das kleine, mobile und multifunktionelle Haus wurde mit Black Box betitelt, da es nach Ansicht des Architekten von außen einem Zauberkasten ähnelt. Die Struktur besteht aus einem einfachen Beleuchtungssystem, hölzernen Rahmen, die ein dreidimensionales Orthogonal for-men, das mit neunzig quadratischen Spanplatten bedeckt wurde. Die Proportionen der Paneele und der Zusammenbau-mechanismus sorgen dafür, dass der Auf- und Abbau ein echtes Kinderspiel bleibt. Das Dach wurde mit einer Membran aus hochwertigem Gummi bedeckt, die das Haus vor Wind und Wet-ter schützt. Das Innere besteht aus einem mittelgroßen, zweige-schossigem Raum. Eine offene Fläche im oberen Geschoss dient als Schlaf- oder Arbeitsbereich. Darunter sind dann Küche, Badezimmer und Treppenhaus eingerichtet, letzteres an der Seite des Kubus.

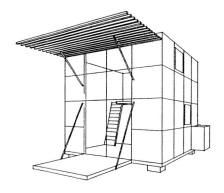

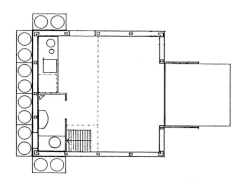

Plan Plan Grundriss

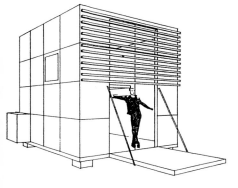

Perspective Perspective Perspektivzeichnung

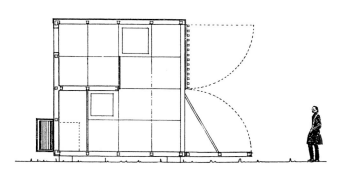

Elevation Élévation Aufriss

The wooden surfaces and pale colors indoors contrast with the exterior to create a warm, inviting atmosphere.

Les surfaces boisées et les teintes pâles de l'intérieur contrastent avec l'extérieur en créant une ambiance chaleureuse et accueillante.

Die Holzflächen und bleichen Farben im Inneren kontrastieren mit dem Äußeren, um eine warme, einladende Atmosphäre zu schaffen.

The building's proportions and the arrangement of the exterior walls are all a function of the structural system; the square form of the chipboard panels emphasizes the contours of the hous

Les proportions de la construction et l'agencement des murs extérieurs font tous partie du système structural. La forme carrée des panneaux de bois aggloméré définit les contours de la maiso

Gebäudeproportionen und Anordnung der Außenwände gehören zur Struktur, die Quadratform der Spanplatten betont die Konturen.

House in Torrelles
Maison à Torrelles
Haus in Torrelles

Rob Dubois

This tiny house with a vertical design, on the outskirts of Barcelona, was placed very close to the road on the northern end of the lot, mitigating its impact on the terrain. This step minimized the amount of excavation required and compressed the building as much as possible, creating a minimal visual impact on the surroundings. The geometry of the building is based on two wedges framing a rectangle. Located at the ends of the house, these wedges are used for the kitchen and bathrooms, while the rectangle includes the living room and bedrooms. The formal language of the house is enriched by the relationship between the rectilinear shapes of the central unit and the curves at the ends. Aligning the main rooms with the longitudinal axis of the plot allowed for long, sweeping views of the immediate area and the valley to the north. The house has three floors which connect the lower and upper levels of the site.

Cette maison minuscule, au design vertical, de la banlieue de Barcelone, est située à la lisière de la rue et à l'extrémité nord du site pour minimiser l'impact sur le terrain. Cette démarche permet de réduire l'importance des travaux d'excavation nécessaires et de comprimer l'édifice au maximum, diminuant ainsi son impact visuel sur l'environnement. La géométrie de base de l'édifice est constituée d'un rectangle encadré de deux empiètements cunéiformes. Construits au bout de la maison, ces empiètements sont utilisés pour la cuisine et les salles de bains, tandis que le salon et les chambres sont intégrés au rectangle. Le jeu qui s'instaure entre les formes rectilignes de l'unité centrale et les courbes des extrémités enrichit le langage formel de la maison. L'alignement des pièces principales sur l'axe longitudinal du terrain permet d'élargir la vue sur les abords immédiats et le nord de vallée. La maison possède trois étages qui relient les niveaux inférieur et supérieur du site.

Dieses kleine Haus in einem Vorort von Barcelona wurde am nördlichen Ende eines Wohnviertels errichtet und fügt sich so wunderbar in die umgebende Landschaft ein. Dadurch konnten auch die Ausgrabungsarbeiten auf ein Mindestmaß reduziert, und das Gebäude an sich so klein wie möglich gehalten werden. Die Geometrie des Gebäudes basiert auf zwei Keilen die den Rahmen für ein Rechteck bilden. Diese beiden Keile sind am jeweiligen Ende des Hauses angebracht und werden als Badezimmer und Küche genutzt, während im Quader Wohn- und Schlafzimmer untergebracht sind. Der eher formelle Aspekt des Hauses wird durch die Verbindung der geradlinigen Formen der Zentraleinheit mit den Kurven am jeweiligen Ende unterstrichen. Da die Haupträume des Hauses in die Längsachse des Geländes eingebunden wurden genießt man von den einzelnen Zimmern aus einen atemberaubenden Ausblick auf die Umgebung und das Tal im Norden. Drei Etagen vereinen die obere und untere Ebene des Geländes miteinander.

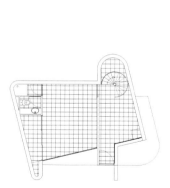

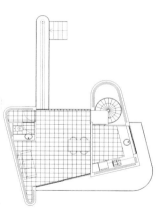

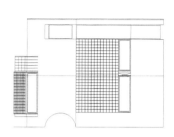

Ground floor Rez-de-chaussée Erdgeschoss

First floor Premier étage Erstes Obergeschoss

Second floor Deuxième étage Zweite Obergeschoss

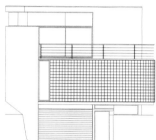

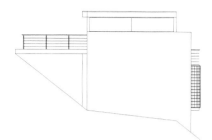

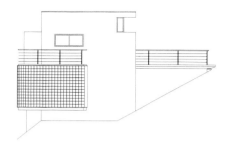

Elevations Élévations Aufrisse

structure built with glass, metal, and concrete contrasts with the rural setting dominated by traditional building materials.

a structure en verre, métal et béton tranche sur l'environnement rural dominé par des matériaux de construction classiques.

n Gebäude aus Glas, Metall und Beton in ländlicher Lage, bei dem traditionelle Baumaterialien den Ton angeben.

The house is enriched by the contrast between the closed surfaces and the large, open spaces set in front of the living and sleeping areas.

La maison est mise en valeur par le contraste entre les surfaces fermées et les grands espaces ouverts du salon et des chambres.

Das Haus besticht durch den Kontrast zwischen der geschlossenen Oberfläche und den großen, offenen Räumen.

The finish of the outer walls, built with glass blocks, combines bright light with a sense of privacy and security.

La finition des murs extérieurs constitués de pavés de verre, décline abondance de lumière, sensation d'intimité et de protection.

Die Oberflächen der Außenwände aus Glasblöcken kombinieren Helligkeit mit einem Gefühl für Privatsphäre und Sicherheit.

House in Senzoku
Maison à Senzoku
Haus in Senzoku

Milligram Studio

This house, located in a quiet residential area in the center of Tokyo, is reminiscent of a flag on first sight. Contrary to this first impression, however, the building's structure has a complicated composition, with five different levels forming the entire living area. The main bedroom is located in the semi-basement so as to ensure the owners' privacy. On the upper level, the occupants can look down from the kitchen area to the lower level, where the living room is situated. Despite the limited space, stairs have been cleverly installed to connect all the levels with the exterior. The architects came up with the simplest method for partitioning spaces by using two long, theater-style drapes. The divisions are enhanced by a high-tech heat-insulation and air-conditioning system that adjusts to the varied, sometimes extreme seasonal weather conditions found in Japan.

Cette maison, implantée dans un quartier résidentiel et calme au centre de Tokyo, rappelle, à première vue, un drapeau. Toutefois, la structure de l'édifice est plus complexe qu'elle ne le parait, la totalité de l'espace de vie étant répartie sur cinq niveaux. Pour préserver l'intimité du propriétaire, la chambre à coucher est située au demi-sous-sol. Depuis la cuisine, installée à l'étage, les occupants ont vue sur le niveau inférieur qui abrite le salon. En dépit d'un espace limité, l'installation judicieuse des escaliers permet de relier tous les niveaux à l'extérieur. Les architectes ont utilisé le cloisonnement de l'espace le plus simple, en utilisant deux longs rideaux de théâtre. Cette partition est rehaussée d'un système high-tech d'isolation thermique et d'air conditionné qui s'adapte aux variations parfois extrêmes des conditions climatiques saisonnières traversées par le Japon.

Dieses Haus befindet sich in einem ruhigen Wohngebiet im Herzen Tokios und ist ein Überbleibsel eines alten Herrenhauses. Unabhängig von dem ersten Eindruck, den es vermittelt, verfügt das Gebäude über eine komplizierte Baustruktur, bei der fünf verschiedne Ebenen den Wohnbereich bestimmen. Das Hauptschlafzimmer ist im Souterrain angelegt um die Privatsphäre des Besitzers zu schützen. Auf der oberen Ebene können die Bewohner auf den Küchenbereich der unteren Ebene blicken, in dem sich auch das Wohnzimmer befindet. Trotz des begrenzten Raums wurden die Treppen so installiert, dass sie tatsächlich alle Ebenen nach außen hin verbinden. Die Architekten haben zwei Theatervorhänge als einfache Methode gewählt um den Raum zu unterteilen. Diese Trennung wird durch eine hochtechnische Thermoisolierung und ein System von Klimaanlagen verstärkt, die den unterschiedlichen, manchmal auch extremen Wetterbedingungen in Japan entsprechen.

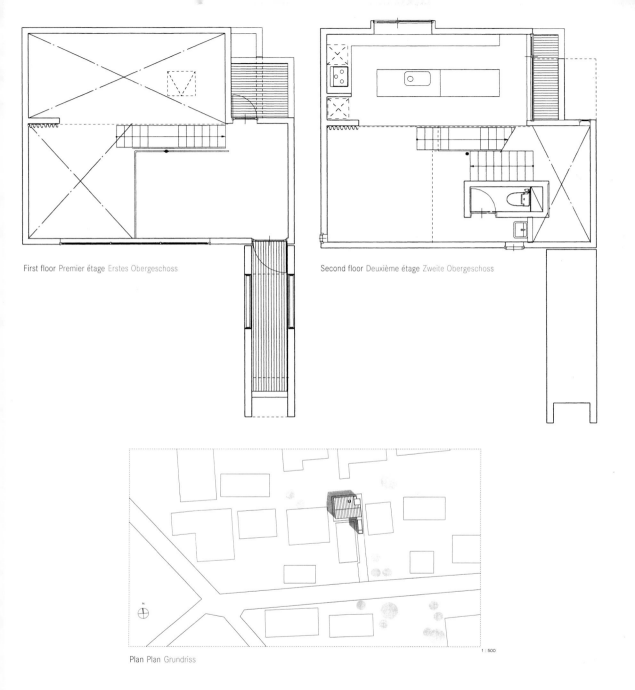

First floor Premier étage Erstes Obergeschoss

Second floor Deuxième étage Zweite Obergeschoss

Plan Plan Grundriss

1 : 500

The impressive approach to the house was realized by taking advantage of the site's unique flag shape.

La conception fantastique de la maison vient de l'optimisation de l'unicité du terrain en forme de drapeau.

Der beeindruckende Ansatz dieses Projekts wurde unter Ausnutzung der einzigartigen Form des Geländes erzielt.

the upper level, the residents can look down from the kitchen area to the lower level, which contains the living room.

étage, les habitants peuvent, depuis la cuisine, contempler le salon situé en contrebas.

der oberen Ebene kann man von der Küche auf die untere Ebene mit dem Wohnzimmer herunterblicken.

☐ Steinhauser House
Maison Steinhauser
Steinhauser Haus

Marte.Marte Architekten

Subjected to the requirement that the house had to blend in with the dock of a navigable canal, the architect was inspired to create a home with a compact structure of aluminum panels with precisely controlled exterior openings. Two large openings on the northern and southern sides break up the metal casing to create a feeling of spaciousness. Inside, the lightweight materials chosen made it possible to build a space that radiates warmth with great speed. Dark red concrete panels cover the floor in the kitchen, and the same color is used for the kitchen furniture and the central area with the fireplace. The bathroom and bedrooms are laid out in a row that comes off a corridor in the western part of the house. Hallways cross the entire space rather than being concentrated at one point. A small loft is accessed by a metal staircase that unfolds at the push of a button, reinforcing the references to nautical engineering.

L'architecte a eu l'idée de créer une habitation dotée d'une structure compacte de panneaux d'aluminium, munis d'ouvertures extérieures réglées par un système de contrôle précis, dans un souci d'harmonie entre la maison et le dock d'un canal navigable. Deux grandes ouvertures au nord et à l'est brisent le caisson en métal créant ainsi une sensation d'espace. A l'intérieur, le choix des matériaux légers engendre un espace très chaleureux. Le sol de la cuisine est recouvert de panneaux de béton rouge foncé, couleur qui se retrouve dans les meubles de cuisine et dans la zone centrale, avec la cheminée. Dans la partie ouest de la maison, la salle de bains et les chambres alignées débouchent sur un couloir. Plutôt que d'être concentrés en un point, les corridors traversent tout l'espace. Par simple pression sur un bouton, un escalier escamotable en acier permet d'accéder à un petit loft, ce qui n'est pas sans rappeler l'aspect nautique de l'ensemble.

Um der Vorgabe zu entsprechen, nach der das Haus sich an den Anleger eines befahrbaren Kanals einfügen sollte, hat der Architekt ein eher kompakt anmutendes Gebäude entworfen, das aus Aluminiumpaneelen besteht und eindeutig abgegrenzte Ausgänge aufweist. Zwei große Öffnungen an der Nord- und Südseite unterbrechen die Metallstruktur um ein Gefühl von Weite zu vermitteln. Im Inneren sorgt das leichtgewichtige Baumaterial dafür, dass man sich hier sofort zuhause fühlt. Dunkelrote Betonplatten bedecken den Küchenboden, dieselbe Farbe wurde auch für die Küchenmöbel und den zentralen Kaminbereich gewählt. Das Badezimmer und die Schlafzimmer wurden nebeneinander in einem Flur am westlichen Teil des Hauses eingerichtet. Gänge führen durch den gesamten Raum und sind nicht so sehr auf einen Punkt konzentriert. Über eine Metalltreppe erreicht man einen Dachboden. Die Treppe wird durch Knopfdruck ausgefahren und verstärkt so das nautische Element des Baus.

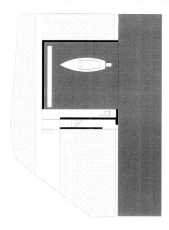

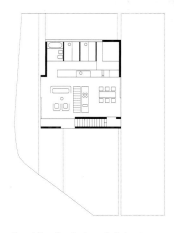

Basement Sous-sol Kellergeschoss   Ground floor Rez-de-chaussée Erdgeschoss

Plan Grundriss

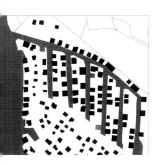

ations Élévations Aufrisse   Section Section Schnitt

A range of housing styles, such as covered cubes, long cabins, rustic 1930s houses, and small tent-like retreats, served as reference points in the design process for this house.

Toute une série de styles d'habitation, à l'instar de cubes couverts, cabines allongées, maison des années 30 et refuges en forme de tente, a servi de critères de référence dans la conception de cette maison.

Hier dienten mehrere Stile als Vorbild, darunter Würfel, Kabinen, rustikale Häuser der 30er Jahre und an Zelte erinnernde Behausungen.

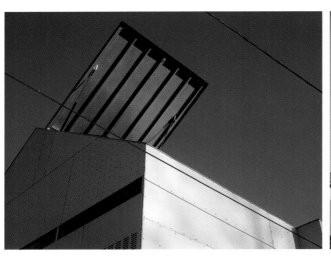

The building's simplicity is enriched by the fine texture of the rivets in the aluminum panels and the striking arrangement of the openings.

La simplicité du bâtiment est rehaussée par la fine texture des rivets des panneaux d'aluminium et l'agencement original des ouvertures.

Die Einfachheit des Gebäudes wird belebt durch die Nieten in den Aluminiumtafeln und die ins Auge fallenden Öffnungen.

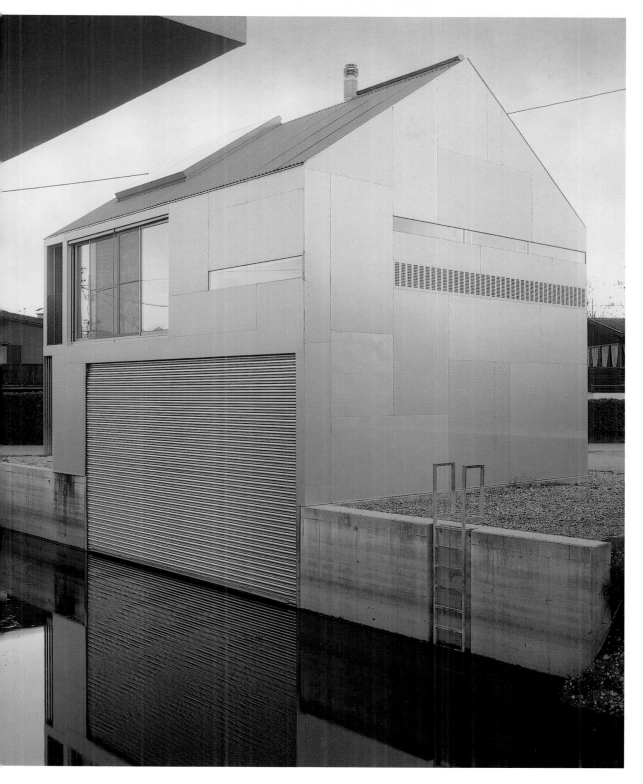

A small loft is accessed via metal stairs, while materials such as plywood and chipboard were used inside to provide a warm atmosphere.

L'accès au petit loft se fait par des escaliers en métal. A l'intérieur, des matériaux comme le contreplaqué et le bois aggloméré dégagent une atmosphère chaleureuse.

Eine Metalltreppe führt in einen kleinen Loft. Innen wurde mit Sperrholz und Spanplatten eine warme Atmosphäre geschaffen.

☐ **Up & Down**
De haut en bas
Hoch und Runter

AV1 Architekten

The theme of this project is architecture versus nature, a concept which stands for all the important decisions taken throughout the planning. A rectangular block of three floors incorporates a series of five houses that parallels the wall of red rock. The sedimentation of natural sandstone was the inspiration for the horizontal larch-wood panel on the north, east and west sides, imitating the layers that are found in the rock. On the south side, the units open onto a meadow and forest with the help of sliding glass elements between wooden frames. Inside, the rooms are wrapped in concrete and a hanging staircase slices through the centre of the three floors. Balconies link the interior to the exterior and also provide protection from the sun during the summer months. The roof integrates a gauge system that stores rainwater in a special layer, draining it through the ground without adding to the municipal sewage, while solar panels heat it up.

Ce projet se décline sur le thème architecture et nature, l'idée maîtresse de la conception. Un bloc rectangulaire de trois étages englobe une série de cinq maisons, à l'instar d'un mur de pierres rouges. Sur les côtés nord, est et sud, le panneau horizontal en bois de mélèze s'inspire de la sédimentation du grès naturel, imitant ainsi les strates de la roche. Sur le côté sud, l'unité s'ouvre sur une prairie et une forêt grâce à des éléments de verre coulissants encastrés dans un châssis de bois. A l'intérieur, les pièces sont enveloppées de béton. Un escalier suspendu glisse au cœur des trois étages. Des balcons, liens entre l'intérieur à l'extérieur, protègent aussi du soleil pendant les mois d'été. Un système de jauge, inséré dans le toit, capte l'eau de pluie dans une assise spéciale, la drainant vers le sol en évitant le tout à l'égout municipal, pour être ensuite réchauffée par des panneaux solaires.

Architektur und Natur: ein Konzept, das bei allen wichtigen Entscheidungen während der Planungsphase Hauses im Vordergrund stand. Ein rechteckiger Kasten mit drei Geschossen umfasst eine Reihe von fünf Häusern, die an einer roten Felswand errichtet wurden. Die Sedimentbildung des natürlichen Sandgesteins diente als Inspiration für die horizontalen Lärchenholzpaneele. Auf der Südseite bieten Glasschiebelementen zwischen hölzernen Rahmen den Blick auf eine Wiese und den Wald. Innen wurden die Räume mit Beton ausgekleidet, und eine hängende Treppenkonstruktion führt durch die Mitte der drei Stockwerke. Verschiedene Balkone verbinden die Innen und Außenräume und dienen in den Sommermonaten auch als Sonnenschutz. Auf dem Dach wurde ein Rohrsystem angebracht, das Regenwasser speichert und in den Grund leitet ohne die örtliche Abwasseranlage zu belasten, während Sonnenkollektoren auf dem Dach den Bau heizen.

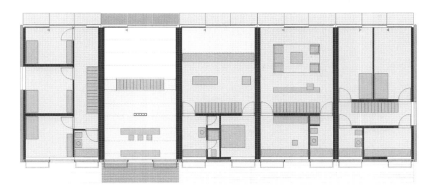

First floor Premier étage Erstes Obergeschoss

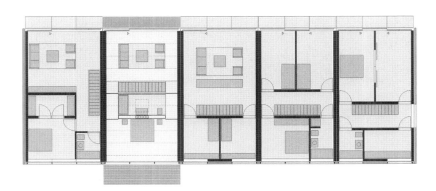

Second floor Deuxième étage Zweite Obergeschoss

The staircase suspended from steel cables becomes an esthetic element that adds a significant dynamic quality to each of the homes.

L'escalier suspendu à des câbles d'acier devient un élément esthétique qui accentue fortement le caractère dynamique de chacune des maisons.

Die an Stahlkabeln hängende Treppe ist ein ästhetisches Element, das für eine zusätzliche Dynamik sorgt.

The kitchen, separated from the dining area by an island unit, opens onto a wooden deck terrace.

La cuisine, séparée de la salle à manger par un îlot de cuisson, s'ouvre sur une terrasse de bois.

Die Küche, die vom Essbereich abgetrennt ist, öffnet sich zu einer Terrasse mit Holzboden.

]

...e interior lighting system, wooden surfaces and pale colors contrast with the concrete used for the ceilings and floors and set up a cozy and welcoming atmosphere.

...système d'éclairage intérieur, les surfaces boisées et les couleurs pâles tranchent sur le béton des plafonds et des sols, créant une atmosphère accueillante et chaleureuse.

...euchtung, Holzflächen und bleiche Farben kontrastieren mit dem Beton der Böden und Decken und schaffen eine warme Atmosphäre.

Cabin at Masía Masnou
Cabane à Masía Masnou
Häuschen in Masía Masnou

Jordi Hidalgo and Daniela Hartmann

This small, simple structured house with a rectangular ground plan and a gabled roof is integrated into the heart of a natural park in the volcanic region of La Garrotxa, Spain. The construction used masonry that combined the local volcanic stone with lime mortar. Three stories sit atop a simple but highly effective supporting structure, which is independent from the original walls and leaves side strips extending on the north and south faces. These strips are covered with movable, laminated glass sheets that act as skylights for the lower story. The brick sections on the first level are broken by large windows, which provide ample light for the living room. Below, a mezzanine contains the kitchen and dining room, while another, on a higher level, accommodates the bedrooms. An outdoor stairway runs up to the main entrance of the house and leads through a hall to the main staircase, which connects all the stories.

La petite maison, simplement conçue, suit un plan rectangulaire, surmonté d'un toit à pignon et se fond au cœur du parc volcanique naturel de la région de La Garrotxa, en Espagne. La construction est faite en maçonnerie qui allie la pierre volcanique et le mortier à base de chaux. Trois étages coiffent une structure simple mais très résistante et du plus bel effet, indépendante des murs d'origine, dotée de bandes latérales le long des façades nord et sud. Ces bandes sont recouvertes de feuilles mobiles de verre laminé, qui transmettent la lumière du jour à l'étage inférieur. Les surfaces en briques du premier étage sont interrompues par de grandes fenêtres, inondant le salon de lumière du jour. En dessous, une mezzanine abrite la cuisine et la salle à manger et à un niveau supérieur, une autre accueille les chambres à coucher. Un escalier extérieur grimpe jusqu'à l'entrée principale de la maison et, au travers d'un hall, mène vers l'escalier principal, trait d'union entre tous les étages.

Dieses kleine, einfach strukturierte Haus mit rechteckigem Grundriss und Giebeldach ist mitten in einen Naturpark in die Vulkanlandschaft von La Garrotxa in Spanien integriert. Beim Bau wurde das örtliche Vulkangestein mit Kalkmörtel zu einer Mauer verbunden. Auf einer einfachen, aber effektiven Stützstruktur wurden drei Etagen errichtet. An der Nord- und Südseite ragen seitliche Verlängerungen über das Haus hinaus. Diese Verlängerungen sind mit beweglichen, laminierten Glaspaneelen bedeckt, die als Oberlicht für das darunter liegende Stockwerk dienen. Die Ziegelwände im ersten Stock werden durch große Fenster unterbrochen. Dadurch fällt ausreichend Licht in das Wohnzimmer ein. Auf einer Zwischenebene wurden darunter Küche und Esszimmer eingerichtet, während auf einer zweiten, etwas höher gelegenen, die Schlafzimmer liegen. Eine Außentreppe führt bis zum Haupteingang und durch einen Flur zur Haupttreppe, die alle drei Stockwerke miteinander verbindet.

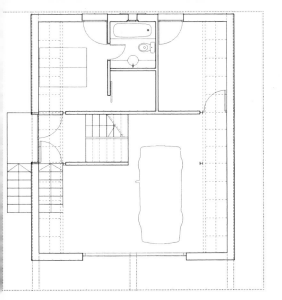

Ground floor Rez-de-chaussée Erdgeschoss

First floor Premier étage Erstes Obergeschoss

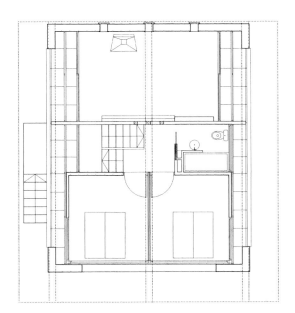

Second floor Deuxième étage Zweite Obergeschoss

The architects sought to create a building that demonstrated conceptual clarity while maximizing the perceptual sensations available from the interior.

Les architectes ont essayé de construire un édifice doté d'une conception claire tout en maximalisant les sensations issues de l'intérieur.

Die Architekten wollten ein Gebäude mit konzeptueller Klarheit und maximalen Sinneswahrnehmungen von Innen schaffen.

A few well-founded decisions produced highly original results - a structure that respects both the environment and the architecture of the original building.

Quelques décisions bien prises qui donnent un résultat très original - une structure qui respecte à la fois l'environnement et l'architecture du bâtiment d'origine.

Richtige Entscheidungen schufen originelle Resultate: Sowohl Umgebung als auch Architektur des Originalhauses werden respektiert.

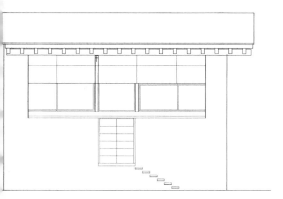

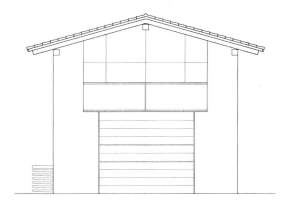

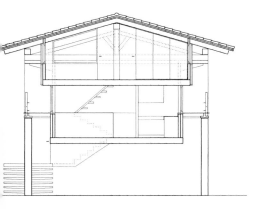

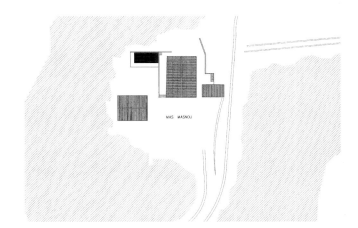

MAS MASNOU

ations Élévations Aufrisse   Plan Plan Grundriss

The supporting structure is a traditional wood truss-rafter arrangement which holds the gable roof and rests on a lattice of beams and metal pillars that underpins the new enclosure.

La structure de soutènement est une poutre classique à chevrons qui soutient le comble à pignon et repose sur des poutres en treillis et des piliers en métal qui étayent la nouvelle construction.

Eine traditionelle Stützstruktur aus Trägern und Sparren trägt das Giebeldach und ruht auf Balken und Metallpfeilern.

ht, transparent design was used for the stairway to accentuate its architectural space and establish a visual relationship between all the areas in the house.

éger design tout en transparence définit l'escalier, exaltant l'espace architectural, tout en établissant une relation visuelle entre les zones de la maison.

Treppe in leichtem, transparentem Design schafft eine Verbindung zwischen allen Bereichen des Hauses.

House in Zachary
Maison à Zachary
Haus in Zachary

Stephen Atkinson

The owners of this plot of Louisiana land, in the midst of a rural landscape of dense oak forest and expansive grassland, decided to build a home for use at weekends or on short vacations. The house is covered by two layers of material: an outer shell that requires little precision in its finishings—it was installed by the owners themselves—protects against the elements, and a more sophisticated inner layer, which required the expertise of skilled workers. While the outer layer consists of a corrugated sheet and fiberglass window panels, the interior finishing of plasterboard and oak provides a touch of warmth. The house consists of two main spaces—a living room and a bedroom—that face each other and are connected by a deck. A long, uninterrupted roof covers both spaces and the deck that cuts across the center of the building. Sliding doors integrate the interior spaces with each other and with the exterior.

Les propriétaires de ce terrain, situé en Louisiane, au cœur d'un paysage rural composé d'une dense forêt de chêne et de vastes prairies, ont décidé de construire une maison de week-ends ou de vacances. Deux couches de matériau recouvrent la maison : une coque externe facile à installer—par les propriétaires eux-mêmes—protège des éléments et une couche interne plus complexe exigeant l'intervention d'ouvriers spécialisés expérimentés. Alors que la coque externe est composée de tôle ondulée et de panneaux de fenêtres en fibre de verre, la finition intérieure en placoplâtre et en chêne apporte une touche de chaleur. La maison est constituée de deux espaces principaux- un salon et une chambre à coucher - qui se font face et sont reliés par une passerelle. Le tout est coiffé d'un long toit couvrant les deux espaces et la passerelle qui traverse le centre du bâtiment. Des portes coulissantes relient les espaces intérieurs entre eux et avec l'extérieur.

Die Besitzer dieses Geländes in Louisiana, das inmitten einer ländlichen Gegend mit alten Eichenbäumen und dichtem Grasland liegt, entschieden sich für den Bau eines Wochenendhauses. Das Gebäude ist mit zwei Lagen Material bedeckt: eine äußere Hülle, die von den Besitzern selbst angebracht wurde und lediglich einen Wetterschutz darstellt und eine aufwendige innere Hülle, die von professionellen Facharbeitern angebracht wurde. Während die äußere Hülle aus Wellblech und Glasfaserfensterpaneelen besteht, wurden die Innenräume mit Gipsplatten und Eiche verkleidet, um ein Gefühl von Wärme zu vermitteln. Das Haus besteht aus zwei Hauptbereichen - einem Wohnzimmer und einem Schlafzimmer - die einander gegenüber liegen und durch ein Deck miteinander verbunden wurden. Ein langes, durchgehendes Dach bedeckt beide Bereiche und das Deck, das in der Mitte des Gebäudes errichtet wurde. Schiebetüren verbinden die einzelnen Bereiche miteinander und führen auch nach außen.

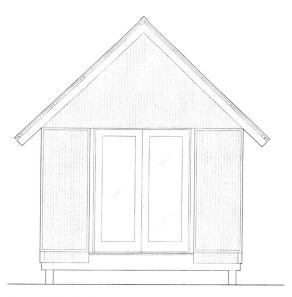

Elevation Élévation Aufriss

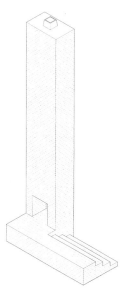

Perspective Perspective Perspektivzeichnung

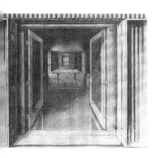

pective Perspective Perspektivzeichnung

Longitudinal section Section longitudinale Längsschnitt

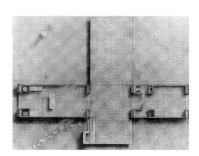

Plan Plan Grundriss

vertical brick structure stands apart from the house; it contains the barbecue and keeps the heat away from the interior.

a structure verticale en briques, à côté de la maison, abrite le barbecue. Elle protège l'intérieur de la chaleur.

ine vertikale Ziegelstruktur steht etwas abseits. Sie beherbergt den Grill und hält die Hitze fern vom Inneren.

The doors and windows are covered with corrugated metal sheeting that seals the house when it is unoccupied.

Les portes et fenêtres sont habillées de feuilles de métal ondulé qui verrouillent la maison lorsqu'elle est inoccupée.

Wenn niemand zuhause ist, wird das Haus mit den Türen und Fenstern aus Wellblech quasi versiegelt.

The austere appearance, bereft of detail, is achieved through the use of a continuous sheet of metal over all the walls and the roof.

L'apparence austère, dépouillée de détails, est obtenue par l'habillage uniforme en métal de tous les murs et du toit.

Das nüchterne Erscheinungsbild wird durch die Wellblechlagen über Mauern und Dach erzeugt.

Interior details and finishing are more refined than those used outdoors, rendering the space comfortable and warm.

étails intérieurs et la finition sont plus raffinés qu'à l'extérieur, dotant l'espace de confort et chaleur.

etails im Inneren sind ausgefeilter als das Außendekor und schaffen eine warme, behagliche Atmosphäre.

House in Flawil
Maison à Flawil
Haus in Flawil

Wespi & De Meuron

Originally one of the first prefabricated wooden structures in Switzerland, this house was transformed and renovated by Wespi & De Meuron Architects into a comfortable home. The project consisted of covering the existing structure with horizontal, wooden slats to create a very tight weave. The new skin covers the house's existing outer walls and stretches out 22 ft to the south, the only direction in which the building could be extended. The service areas, such as the kitchen, stairs, bathroom, and office, are grouped toward the north. Thus, a kind of chamber is created around the most privileged part of the house to protect the living areas. The almost hermetic wooden finish on the northern, eastern, and western sides contributes to the passive solar effect, while the southern side opens up to receive as much heat as possible from the sun. The wooden slats on this side act like blinds to provide protection during the summer months.

Première structure préfabriquée en bois réalisée en Suisse, cette maison a été transformée et restaurée par les architectes Wespi & De Meuron, en une habitation confortable. Le projet était de couvrir la structure existante de lattes de bois horizontales pour créer un treillis très serré. Le nouveau revêtement recouvre les murs extérieurs de la maison et s'étend de 7 mètres vers le sud, seule direction possible pour agrandir la maison. Dans la zone des services, la cuisine, l'escalier la salle de bains et le bureau sont regroupés vers le nord. C'est ainsi qu'une sorte de chambre a été créée autour de la partie la plus privilégiée de la maison pour protéger les pièces à vivre. La finition en bois, renforce l'effet passif du soleil, tandis que la façade sud s'ouvre pour recevoir un maximum de chaleur solaire. Sur ce côté, les lattes de bois font office de volets pour protéger de la chaleur pendant les mois d'été.

Dieses Haus gehört zu den ersten Holzfertighäusern, die in der Schweiz errichtet wurden. Später wurde es dann von den Architekten Wespi & De Meuron renoviert und in ein gemütliches Heim umgebaut. Die bestehende Struktur wurde mit horizontalen Holzlatten verkleidet, um so eine wetterfeste Abdichtung zu schaffen. Diese neue Hülle bedeckt die äußeren Wände des Hauses und erstreckt sich über 7 m nach Süden, die einzige Richtung in die das Haus vergrößert werden konnte. Die Nutzbereiche wie Küche, Treppenhaus, Badezimmer und Büro wurden nach Norden verlegt. Dadurch wurde eine Art Kammer um den schönsten Teil des Hauses gebaut, um den inneren Wohnbereich zu schützen. Der fast hermetische, hölzerne Abschluss an den nördlichen, östlichen und westlichen Seiten tragen zur Wärmedämmung bei, während die Südseite offen bleibt um so viel Sonne wie möglich aufzunehmen. Die Holzlatten auf dieser Seite dienen lediglich als Schutz vor zuviel Sonne während der Sommermonate.

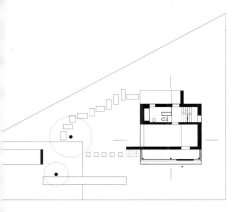

nd floor Rez-de-chaussée Erdgeschoss

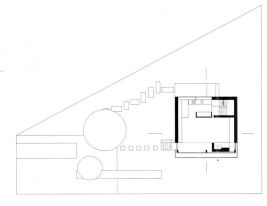

First floor Premier étage Erstes Obergeschoss

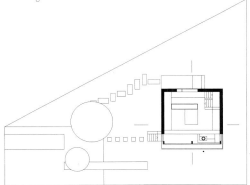

Second floor Deuxième étage Zweite Obergeschoss

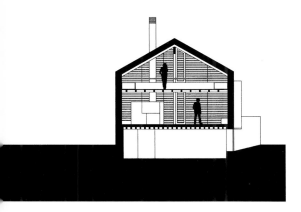

section Section transversale Querschnitt

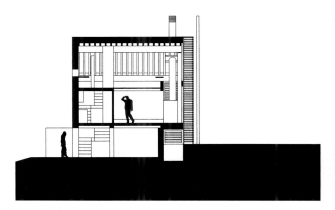

Longitudinal section Section longitudinale Längsschnitt

e strategy for expanding the house was based on the appearance of the local farm buildings.

xtension de cette maison s'est modelée sur l'aspect des fermes de la région.

e Strategie zur Erweiterung dieses Hauses basierte auf dem Erscheinungsbild der lokalen Bauernhäuser.

The wooden slats act like blinds to provide protection from the sun during the summer months.
Les lattes de bois font office de volets qui protègent du soleil d'été.
Die Holzlatten bieten während der Sommermonate Schutz vor der Sonne.

...de and out, the dominant material is wood. This makes for continuity of appearance and a warm, welcoming atmosphere.

...ntérieur comme à l'extérieur, le bois qui domine sur les autres matériaux, unit l'ensemble et lui confère une ambiance chaleureuse et accueillante.

...en und außen dominiert Holz als Baumaterial. Dies schafft eine warme, einladende Atmosphäre.

☐ Heidi House
Maison Heidi
Heidi Haus

Matteo Thun

The architect Matteo Thun took on the enormous challenge of designing a prefabricated house that would go beyond the simple notion of a cabin and occupy its surroundings with the utmost delicacy and subtlety. A detailed study of the site enabled the designer to create a structure that was suited to the mountainous landscape while being in keeping with the region's traditional architecture. The structure is rectangular, composed along elementary lines, and topped with a roof reminiscent of the large-span structures typically seen in barns. The outside walls have a laminated wooden skin, while shutters, also made of wood, filter the sunlight entering the house and unify the language of the building. The south face has been opened up by large windows that look out onto the spectacular landscape and ensure that as much sunshine as possible enters the house during the winter. The walls are thermally insulated with cork panels, protecting the house against the rough mountain climates.

L'architecte Matteo Thun a relevé l'énorme défi de concevoir une maison préfabriquée qui dépasse la simple notion de cabane en s'intégrant dans le paysage avec une finesse et une subtilité extrêmes. Grâce à une étude détaillée du site, le designer a créé une structure adaptée au paysage montagneux tout en respectant l'architecture traditionnelle de la région. Rectangulaire, la structure de conception linéaire est coiffée d'un toit rappelant les toitures à large travée des fermes traditionnelles. Les murs extérieurs sont recouverts de bois laminé, les volets également en bois, filtrent la lumière du soleil pénétrant la maison et unifient l'expression architecturale du bâtiment. De larges baies vitrées ouvrent la façade sud sur un paysage spectaculaire laissant la lumière du soleil pénétrer à flots pendant l'hiver. Des panneaux de liège assurent l'isolation thermique, protégeant la maison de la rudesse du climat de montagne.

Der Architekt Matteo Thur wollte ein kleines Haus entwerfen, das dabei aber nicht einfach nur einer Hütte ähneln, sondern sich geschickt in die Umgebung einfügen sollte. Es gelang dem Designer einen Entwurf vorzulegen, der nicht nur der umgebenden Berglandschaft entspricht, sondern sich auch an die traditionelle Bauweise der Region anpasst. Die Struktur ist recheckig und besteht aus elementaren Linien, die mit einem Dach gekrönt wurden, die an die großen und weiten Dachstühle einer Scheune erinnert. Die äußeren Wände wurden mit Holzlaminat verkleidet, während Fensterläden, die ebenfalls aus Holz gefertigt wurden, den Einfall des Sonnenlichtes in das Haus filtern und den Gesamteindruck des Hauses verstärken. In die Südseite wurden große Fenster eingebaut, die auf die herrliche Landschaft hinausweisen und dafür sorgen, dass im Winter so viel Sonnenlicht wie möglich in das Haus fällt. Die Wände wurden mit Korkplatten isoliert und schützen die Innenräume vor dem rauhen Bergklima.

The design permits the adaptation of the structure to each client's needs, so that a wide variety of options can be achieved from one basic concept.

Grâce au design, la structure s'adapte au gré des désirs des clients selon un concept de base offrant une multitude d'options.

Die Struktur kann an die Anforderungen jedes Kunden angepasst werden. Das Basisdesign bietet eine Vielzahl an Variationen.

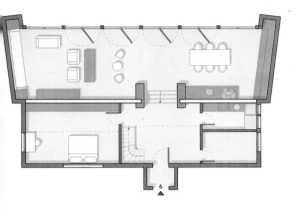

Ground floor Rez-de-chaussée Erdgeschoss

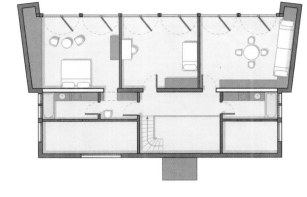

First floor Premier étage Erstes Obergeschoss

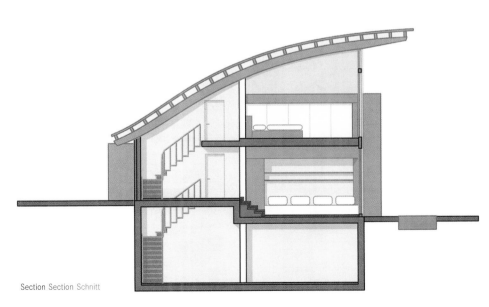

Section Section Schnitt

Cross-section of Heidi house showing the different stories, the vaulted roof, and the basement, which functions as a structural support.

Coupe de la maison Heidi House montrant les différents étages, la voûte du toit et le sous-sol qui fait office de support structurel.

Querschnitt vom Heidi Haus. Zu sehen sind die Stockwerke, das Dach und der Keller, der als Stütze dient.

This house is noteworthy on account of the enormously thick walls rising from the ground, the abundance of laminated wood surfaces, and the solid wood beams that support the wide roof section.

Cette maison se distingue par l'épaisseur considérable de ses murs surgissant du sol, l'abondance des surfaces en bois contreplaqué et par des poutres très solides soutenant toute la largeur du toit.

Hier fallen besonders die dicken Wände, die Holzoberflächen und die soliden Holzbalken auf. Letztere stützen das weite Dach.

...ules can be incorporated into the structure of the house to provide either more bedrooms or larger communal areas, all within a simple ground plan.
...modules peuvent être intégrés à la structure de la maison pour augmenter le nombre de chambres ou pour élargir les aires communes à partir d'un plan de base très simple.
...ule können in die Struktur aufgenommen werden, um zusätzliche Schlafzimmer oder Wohnbereiche hinzuzufügen.

...n a slightly lower level, an extensive space containing the living room, dining room, and kitchen looks out through large windows on to the beautiful, mountainous landscape.
...ur un niveau légèrement en contrebas, une grande surface héberge le salon, la salle à manger et la cuisine, s'ouvrant grâce à de grandes baies vitrées, sur le paysage montagneux.
...Weiter unten befindet sich ein ausgedehnter Raum mit Wohn- & Esszimmer und Küche. Der Blick geht hinaus auf die Berglandschaft.

☐ **Studio 3773**

Dry Design

This extraordinary project involves a former garage in a Californian neighborhood that was transformed into a small studio and home for the architects' own use. Different planes on different levels accommodate the various household functions and enrich the interior space. The first plane, which comprises the ground floor, is a polished concrete slab where a lot of activity takes place. In the main unit, the kitchen, dining room, living room, and studio share a common space, while a small adjacent unit contains the bathroom. Another, intermediate plane, suspended by a framework hanging from the ceiling, is a wooden loft containing the bed. A roof and small garden above the bathroom make up a final, exterior plane. The relationship between the interior and exterior, like the relationships between the various spaces, was designed to achieve maximum flexibility. Thus, the building can be used as a studio, guest apartment, or independent home.

Ce projet extraordinaire s'articule autour d'un ancien garage dans un coin de Californie, transformé en un petit studio et lieu d'habitation pour l'architecte lui-même. Différents plans et niveaux s'adaptent aux multiples fonctions de la maison et enrichissent l'espace intérieur. Le premier plan, comprenant le rez-de-chaussée –une dalle de béton poli– est le lieu d'une multitude d'activités. Dans l'unité centrale, cuisine, salle à manger, salon et un studio se partagent l'espace, avec une petite unité adjacente où se trouve la salle de bains. Un autre plan intermédiaire, fait d'une structure suspendue au plafond, est constitué d'un loft avec un lit. Un toit et un petit jardin coiffent la salle de bains, créant un dernier plan extérieur. Le lien entre l'intérieur et l'extérieur et celui qui existe entre les divers espaces, ont été conçu dans un souci de flexibilité maximale. Au gré des besoins, l'habitation peut se transformer en studio, appartement d'invité ou logement indépendant.

Hier wurde eine ehemalige Garage in Kalifornien in ein kleines Studio und ein Zuhause für den Architekten umgewandelt. Die einzelnen Zimmer sind auf unterschiedlichen Ebenen angebracht, was den Innenraum optisch vergrößert. Das Erdgeschoss besteht aus einer polierten Betonplatte, die viel Raum für Aktivitäten bietet. Der Hauptwohnteil mit der Küche, dem Esszimmer, Wohnzimmer und einem Studio sind auf einer weiteren Ebene untergebracht, während das Badezimmer in einem kleinen Anbau eingerichtet wurde. Eine mittlere Ebene wurde von der Decke abgehängt und besteht aus einem aus Holz gefertigten Hochbett. Ein Dach und ein kleiner Garten über dem Badezimmer bilden eine weitere Ebene im Außenbereich. Die einzelnen Verbindungen zwischen dem Innen- und Außenraum, sowie die Beziehung zwischen den einzelnen Räumen wurden so gestaltet, dass eine maximale Flexibilität ermöglicht wird. Das Gebäude kann daher sowohl als Studio, Gästehaus, aber auch als allein stehendes Haus genutzt werden.

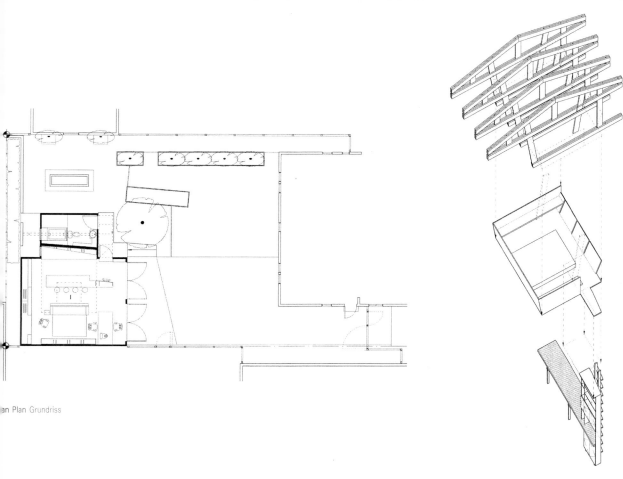

an Plan Grundriss

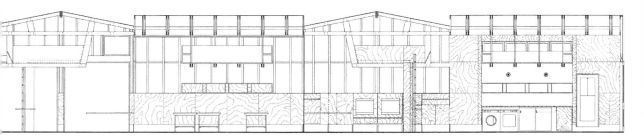

vation Élévation Aufriss

n independent unit, suspended by a framework hanging from the ceiling, serves as a wooden loft containing the bed.

ne unité indépendante, suspendue par une structure accrochée au plafond, fait office de loft en bois doté d'un lit.

as Bett steht auf einer unabhängigen Einheit aus Holz, die an einem Rahmen unter der Decke hängt.

Although this home backs on to another house, the garden surrounding it creates a charming, private setting.

Bien que mitoyenne, cette maison est entourée d'un jardin créant un cadre privé charmant.

Dieses Haus grenzt zwar an ein anderes Haus, der Garten rundherum schafft jedoch ein angenehmes Gefühl von Abgeschiedenheit.

All the interior surfaces are made of plywood panels to ensure good insulation and a rich texture.

Toutes les surfaces intérieures sont faites de panneaux en contreplaqué parfaitement isolant et de belle texture.

Alle Innenflächen sind aus Sperrholz. Dies sorgt für gute Isolierung und abwechslungsreiche Muster.

☐ Office House
Maison et bureau
Bürohaus

Desai/Chia Studio

This small house was placed in the middle of an isolated area, densely populated with trees, away from the urban bustle and its immediate neighbors to accommodate a financial consultant who needed to work in comfort. The basic plan divides the structure into two floors, to avoid taking up too much land and to fully enjoy the views of the surrounding woods. The ground floor includes parking for two cars, a gym, and a fully equipped bathroom, while the upper floor is reserved for the main living area, the office, and the library. The building was conceived as a simple box, integrated into its natural setting. Strips of windows appear on the façade in different patterns, framing different views of the landscape. On the ground floor, windows emphasizing the landscape's verticality of the landscape look out on the woods, while on the upper floor, light from the north reaches the high windows, filtered through the leaves.

Cette petite maison a été construite au cœur d'une région isolée, très arborée, à l'écart de l'agitation urbaine et du voisinage immédiat, à la requête d'un consultant financier soucieux de travailler dans le calme. Le plan de base divise la structure en deux étages pour éviter d'envahir trop le terrain et de jouir totalement de la vue sur les bois environnants. Le rez-de-chaussée comprend un garage pour deux voitures, une salle de gymnastique et une salle de bains entièrement équipée. L'étage est réservé à l'espace de vie principal, le bureau et la bibliothèque. L'édifice conçu comme une simple boîte, s'intègre au paysage naturel. La façade est dotée de fenêtres en forme de bandes de différents formats, encadrant diverses vues du paysage. Au rez-de-chaussée, les fenêtres donnant sur les bois, accentuent la verticalité du paysage. A l'étage, les baies vitrées en hauteur reçoivent la lumière du Nord, filtrée à travers le feuillage.

Dieses kleine Haus wurde inmitten eines mit Bäumen bewachsenen Grundstücks errichtet. Weit entfernt von dem Lärm der Großstadt und den Nachbarn hat hier ein Finanzberater sein Zuhause und sein Heimbüro eingerichtet. Der Grundriss teilt die Struktur in zwei Etagen um nicht zuviel Grundfläche in Anspruch zu nehmen und gleichzeitig den herrlichen Blick auf die umgebenden Wälder zu erhalten. Im Erdgeschoss befinden sich eine Garage mit 2 Stellplätzen, ein Fitnessraum, sowie ein voll ausgestattetes Badezimmer. Oben ist dagegen Raum für das Wohnzimmer, das Büro und die Bibliothek. Das Gebäude wurde als einfacher Quader entworfen, der sich perfekt in die natürliche Umgebung einpasst. In der Fassade sind verschiedene Fenster angebracht, die den Rahmen für unterschiedliche Ausblicke auf die Landschaft bilden. Im Erdgeschoss verstärken die Fenster den vertikalen Ausblick auf die bewaldete Umgebung, im Obergeschoss fällt das Licht durch die Blätter der umgebenden Bäume ein.

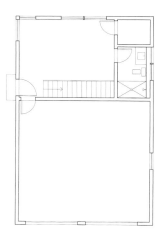

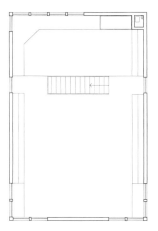

Ground floor Rez-de-chaussée Erdgeschoss

First floor Premier étage Erstes Obergeschoss

Longitudinal section Section longitudinale Längsschnitt

Cross section Section transversale Querschnitt

y treating the wooden outer shell as if it were a piece of furniture, the architect took full advantage of each element, on the basis of its dimensions and physical properties.

n traitant l'ossature en bois extérieure comme un meuble, l'architecte a tiré parti de chaque élément à partir de ses dimensions et propriétés physiques.

ie Außenhaut aus Holz wurde quasi als Möbelstück behandelt. Der Architekt nutzte buchstäblich jedes Bauelement.

The interior details are simple and austere, reinforcing the idea of a quiet refuge in the woods.

Les détails intérieurs sont simples et austères, soulignant l'idée d'un havre de paix entouré de bois.

Die Details im Inneren sind einfach und nüchtern und verstärken den Eindruck einer Zuflucht in den Wäldern.

☐ Arrowleaf House
Maison Arrowleaf
Arrowleaf Haus

James Cutler

The aim of this project was to construct a small, modest building that would respect the natural environment while providing all the comforts of a home. The building is raised off the ground by ten reinforced concrete pillars. The house that stands on this base slab is essentially a box with a gable roof, both made of wood. The base has two openings: One on the southern side provides access to the interior while a larger one on the northern side opens onto a terrace with a panoramic view. The interior is a simple layout on two levels. Entering the lower section, the kitchen, dining room, and living room, are all laid out in a single space. The second level contains the bathroom and the two bedrooms, one of which is enclosed while the other opens out directly onto the living room. The bath and toilet, the stairway, and part of the furniture take up the lateral walls, freeing the interior space and focusing attention on the exit to the terrace.

Le but de ce projet était de construire une petite maison modeste, respectant l'environnement et dotée de tout le confort nécessaire. La construction est posée sur dix piliers en béton armé qui la surélèvent ainsi du sol. La maison assise sur ce socle, a la forme d'une boîte avec un comble sur pignon tout en bois. La base comprend deux ouvertures : une sur le côté sud qui permet d'accéder à l'intérieur et une autre, plus large, sur le côté nord qui donne sur une terrasse avec une vue panoramique. Le plan intérieur est simple et s'articule sur deux niveaux. Au niveau inférieur, la cuisine, la salle à manger et le salon occupent un espace unique. Le niveau supérieur abrite la salle de bains et deux chambres, l'une fermée et l'autre ouverte directement sur le salon. Salle de bains, toilettes, escalier et une partie du mobilier sont disposés le long des murs latéraux, libérant ainsi l'espace intérieur pour que les regards convergent vers le point de mire : la terrasse.

Ziel dieses Projektes war ein kleines, eher bescheiden anmutendes Gebäude zu erbauen, das sich nahtlos in die umgebende Landschaft einfügt und dennoch den Anforderungen an ein gemütliches Heim entspricht. Das Gebäude wird von zehn verstärkten Betonpfeilern getragen und auf dieser Erhöhung wurde dann ein Kasten mit einem Giebeldach aus Holz errichtet. Die Basis verfügt über 2 Ausgänge. Eine Tür am südlichen Ende bietet Zugang zum Innenraum, während eine zweite Tür an der Nordseite auf eine Terrasse mit Panoramablick führt. Das Innere des Hauses ist einfach und in zwei Ebenen gehalten. Im unteren Bereich sind Küche, Ess- und Wohnzimmer im selben Raum untergebracht. Oben befinden sich Badezimmer und zwei Schlafzimmer,eines davon in sich abgeschlossen, das zweite öffnet sich zum Wohnzimmer. Badezimmer und WC, das Treppenhaus und ein Teil der Möbel befinden sich an der hinteren Wand und schaffen so Raum. Der Blick wird auf den Ausgang zur Terrasse gelenkt.

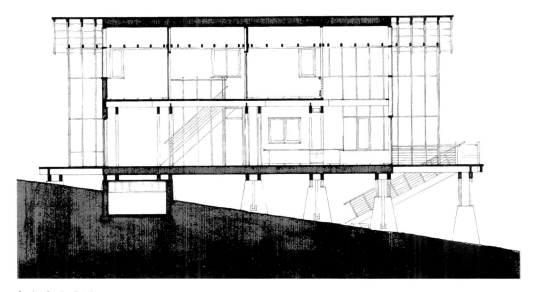

Section Section Schnitt

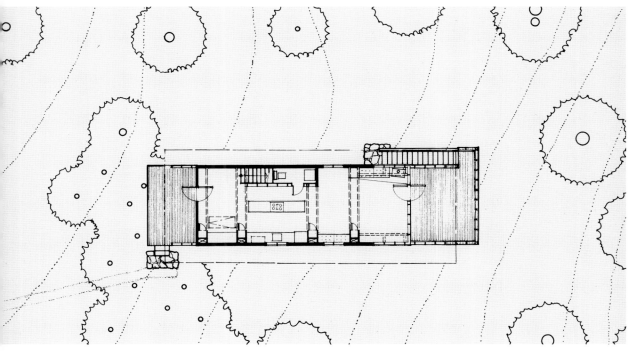

Plan Grundriss

The exterior surface has been carefully finished with thin wood strips to create a delicate visual texture.

Composée de fines lamelles de bois, la finition de la surface extérieure est très soignée, créant une texture optique tout en subtilité.

Das Haus wurde außen liebevoll mit dünnen Holzstreifen verkleidet und wirkt dadurch eher zierlich.

A stairway descends from the terrace to the ground, where a path leads straight into the forest.

Un escalier descend directement de la terrasse vers le sol où un chemin mène à la forêt.

Eine Treppe führt von der Terrasse zum Boden, von dort aus führt ein Pfad direkt in den Wald.

☐ Small House
Petit maison
Kleines Haus

Bauart Architekten

This project, promoted by Architectureforsale, is a prefabricated home that can be set up anywhere and is adaptable to different needs, like the extension of a growing family's home, an independent house for one person, or a private office. Versatility, ease of transport, and simple assembly were the project's main objectives. The home is a small container with regular rectangular proportions, optimized for maximum spatial and functional efficiency. Each of the four outside walls has a large window connecting the space to the surroundings while providing natural light and ventilation to all the rooms. The structure consists of a system of prefabricated wooden frames finished with wooden panels and strips. The foundations, also prefabricated, can be assembled on site, and the whole house can be put up in a single day. Moreover, the carefully planned structure and the dimensions of the building allow it to be moved anywhere. In short, it is a simple but very comfortable home.

Ce projet, promu par le bureau Architectureforsale, est une habitation préfabriquée qui peut être installée partout au gré des besoins : agrandissement d'une maison de famille, maison individuelle pour une personne ou bureaux privés. Polyvalence, facilité de transport et d'assemblage sont les principaux atouts du projet. La maison est un petit container aux dimensions rectangulaires, optimisé pour obtenir un maximum d'efficacité fonctionnelle et spatiale. Chacun des quatre murs extérieurs dispose d'une grande fenêtre, lien entre l'espace et l'environnement et, en même temps, source de lumière naturelle et de ventilation pour toutes les pièces. L'ossature se compose d'un système de châssis de bois préfabriqués, recouverts de panneaux et de lattes de bois. Les fondations, également préfabriquées, peuvent être assemblées sur place et la maison entière est constructible en une journée. Grâce à sa structure parfaitement étudiée et à ses dimensions, elle peut être déplacée partout. En bref, c'est une maison simple mais très confortable.

Dieses Projekt von Architectureforsale handelt sich um ein Fertighaus, das individuellen Vorgaben angepasst werden kann. So dient es z.B. als Anbau für ein bestehendes Haus, kann aber auch als allein stehendes Haus für eine Einzelperson oder als privates Büro genutzt werden. Vielseitigkeit, einfacher Transport und leichter Aufbau. Bei dem Haus handelt es sich um einen kleinen Container mit regelmäßigen Proportionen, die Raum und Funktionalität aufs Beste miteinander verbinden. Jede der vier Außenwände weist ein großes Fenster auf und sorgt somit für natürliches Tageslicht und Belüftung in allen Räumen. Die Struktur besteht aus einem System aus vorgefertigten Holzrahmen, die mit hölzernen Paneelen und Leisten verstärkt wurden. Das Fundament kann vor Ort zusammengesetzt werden, die gut durchdachte Struktur und die Abmessungen des Gebäudes ermöglichen es, dieses Haus an einem einzigen Tag aufzuschlagen. Ein einfaches, aber gemütliches Haus.

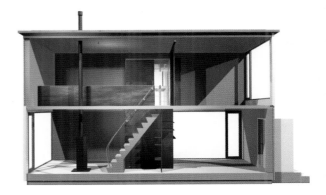

Longitudinal sections Sections longitudinales Längsschnitte

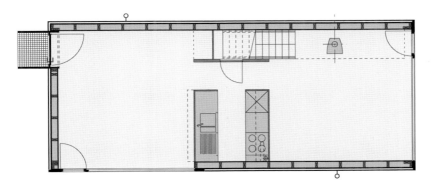

Ground floor Rez-de-chaussée Erdgeschoss

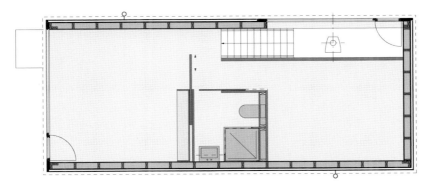

First floor Premier étage Erstes Obergeschoss

The large windows ensure a close relationship with the exterior while making the interior seem much bigger.

Les baies vitrées établissent un lien étroit avec l'extérieur, tout en accentuant l'impression d'espace intérieur.

Die großen Fenster sorgen für eine enge Verbindung nach außen und lassen das Innere größer erscheinen.

The main challenge was to create a compact home with prefabricated components that would be easy to put together but very comfortable and adaptable to different needs.

Le défi à relever était de créer une maison compacte, en éléments préfabriqués facilement mis en place, confortables et adaptables aux divers besoins.

Die Herausforderung bestand darin, ein kompaktes, vielseitiges und wohnliches Haus aus vorgefertigten Komponenten zu bauen.

materials on the outer structure are also used indoors to create a warm, comfortable atmosphere.

matériaux utilisés pour la structure extérieure se retrouvent à l'intérieur pour procurer une atmosphère chaleureuse et confortable.

außen verwendeten Materialien werden ebenfalls innen verwendet und schaffen eine warme, wohnliche Atmosphäre.

Tree House
Cabane
Baumhaus

Dawson Brown Architecture

The idea behind the extension of this 1920s summer house was to preserve the values of the existing structure and its natural setting as much as possible. The owners found the space insufficient, even for a temporary residence, and decided to enlarge it. After studying several possibilities, the architects arrived at a plan in which the extension, a small, slender wooden construction, would be separate from the main building, like a tree house. This independence made it possible to preserve the scale of the existing house and create a structure with its own personality. Although the materials used are similar to those of the original house, the final result is very different and the verticality that predominates in the new building contrasts with the horizontal composition of the old one. The cabin can be reached via stairs from the ground or a terrace at its base that extends from the old house.

L'agrandissement de cette maison d'été des années 20, repose sur l'idée de conserver les valeurs structurelles existantes et de l'environnement naturel autant que faire se peut. Jugeant l'espace insuffisant, même pour une résidence secondaire, les propriétaires ont entrepris de l'agrandir. Après avoir étudié plusieurs possibilités, les architectes ont opté pour la conception d'une petite construction élancée en bois, séparée du bâtiment principal, à l'instar d'une cabane dans un arbre. Cette unité indépendante a permis de garder l'échelle de la maison existante et de créer une structure différente. Bien que les matériaux utilisés soient les mêmes que ceux de la maison d'origine, le résultat final est très différent. En effet, la verticalité, qui est l'âme du nouveau bâtiment, tranche avec la composition horizontale de l'ancien. Un escalier partant du sol ou d'une terrasse reliée à l'ancienne maison par une extension, permet d'accéder à la cabane.

Die Idee hinter dem Ausbau dieses Sommerhauses aus den 20er Jahren war es, die vorgegebene Struktur und ihre natürliche Einbindung so weit als möglich zu erhalten. Die Besitzer benötigten mehr Platz und entschieden sich dafür, das Gebäude zu vergrößern. Nachdem verschiedene Möglichkeiten durchgespielt wurden haben die Architekten einen Plan vorgelegt, bei dem ein kleiner, aus Holz gestalteter Anbau separat vom Hauptgebäude errichtet werden würde, der einem Baumhaus ähnelt. Diese Trennung sorgt dafür, dass die Abmessung des bestehenden Hauses erhalten, gleichzeitig aber eine Struktur mit ganz eigener Charakteristik gebaut werden konnte. Obwohl das verwendete Material dem des Originalhauses gleicht unterscheidet das Ergebnis sich jedoch entscheidend davon, und die senkrechte Lage des neuen Gebäudes kontrastiert mit der horizontalen Zusammenstellung des alten. Man erreicht diese Hütte über eine Treppe vom Boden oder einer Terrasse aus, die vom alten Gebäude abgeht.

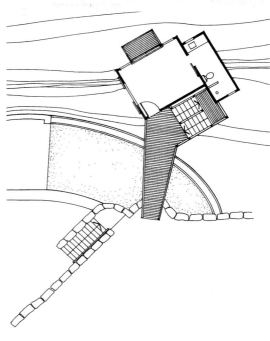

Ground floor Rez-de-chaussée Erdgeschoss

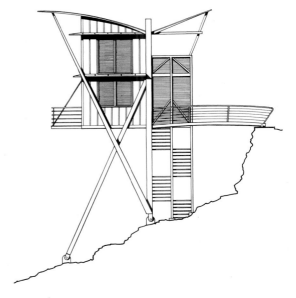

Elevation Élévation Aufriss

The new building took advantage of the views of the surrounding forest and the open sea previously unavailable to the pre-existing house.

La nouvelle construction a optimisé les vues sur la forêt environnante et sur la mer, inexistantes dans la maison antérieure.

Der Neubau nutzte den Ausblick auf den Wald und das offene Meer, die vom vorherigen Haus aus nicht zu sehen waren.

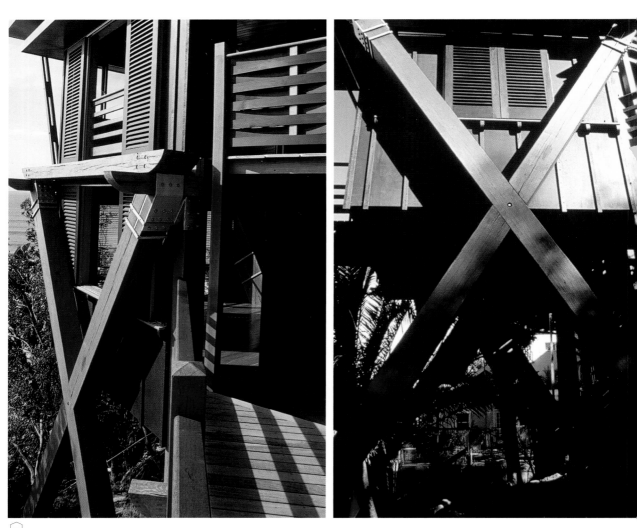

The tree house, made of wooden components anchored with metal parts, was built with special care to minimize the impact on its natural setting.

La cabane, faite d'éléments de bois accrochés par des fixations de métal, a été construite en minimisant son impact sur la nature.

Das Baumhaus aus mit Metallteilen befestigten Holzkomponenten passt sich perfekt in die Natur der Umgebung ein.

verticality predominant in the new building contrasts with the old house's horizontal composition.

erticalité qui caractérise la nouvelle construction, tranche avec l'horizontalité de l'ancienne maison.

ikalität dominiert in dem Neubau und bildet einen interessanten Kontrast zu der horizontalen Anlage des alten Gebäudes.

☐ Refraction House
Maison Réfraction
Refraktionshaus

Kiyoshi Sey Takeyama

The construction of single-person houses has become very common in Japan and these spaces tend to be elongated, continuous and open-plan. This house was commissioned by the owner of a restaurant and built in a typical residential area on the outskirts of Nagoya. Its outer shell is entirely composed of inclined metallic casing, with zinc sides and façades in oxidized steel. A rectangular concrete tower at the back balances the main areas, which are linked by a glass passageway. While the main space contains the residence, the lower floor of the tower is dedicated to receiving guests. The guest bathroom is located on the upper floors. The walls of these areas are painted white, while the floors feature a variety of materials: ceramic tiles, wooden panels, tatami mats, polished concrete, and bamboo canes. Individual elements such as the slanted columns and the long walkways emphasize the simplicity and strength with which this residence is built.

Au Japon, il est monnaie courante de construire des maisons pour une personne : espaces souvent allongés, conçus selon un plan ouvert et fluide. Cette maison, commandité par le propriétaire d'un restaurant, est construite dans un quartier résidentiel typique de la banlieue de Nagoya. La coque extérieure est entièrement composée d'un manteau métallique oblique, doté de côtés en zinc et de façades en acier oxydé. A l'arrière, la tour de béton fait contrepoids à l'espace principal abritant la résidence et y est reliée par une passerelle en verre. L'étage inférieur de la tour est consacré aux invités. Leur salle de bains se trouve à l'étage supérieur. Les murs blancs de ces espaces tranchent avec les sols aux matériaux divers : tuiles en céramique, panneaux boisés, tapis tatami, béton poli et bambous. Des éléments isolés à l'instar des colonnes obliques et des longs passages soulignent la simplicité et la rigueur qui émanent de la construction.

Der Bau von Häusern für Einzelpersonen ist in Japan inzwischen sehr verbreitet und diese Räume sind in der Regel gestreckt, durchgängig und offen. Das Haus wurde von dem Besitzer eines Restaurants in einem Vorort von Nagoya errichtet. Die äußere Hülle wurde ganz aus schrägen Metallplatten gefertigt, die Seiten aus Zink und die Fassade aus oxidiertem Stahl. Ein rechteckiger Betonturm im hinteren Teil unterbricht die Hauptwohnbereiche, die durch einen gläsernen Flur miteinander verbunden sind. Während im größeren Bereich das eigentliche Haus untergebracht ist, dient das Untergeschoss des Turms als Gästezimmer. Das Gästebad liegt oben. Die Wände dieser Bereiche sind weiß gestrichen, während die Böden eine Reihe von Materialien aufweisen: Keramikfliesen, Holzpaneele, Tatamimatten, polierter Beton und Bambusrohre. Einzelne Elemente, wie z.B. die abgeschrägten Säulen und langen Flure unterstützen den Eindruck von Klarheit und Stärke.

e outer shell is entirely composed of an inclined metallic siding, with the sides in zinc and the façades in oxidized steel.

a coque extérieure est entièrement habillée de métal incliné. Les côtés sont en zinc et la façade en acier oxydé.

as Äußere besteht aus einer geneigten Metallverkleidung. Die Seiten sind aus Zink und die Fassade aus oxidiertem Stahl.

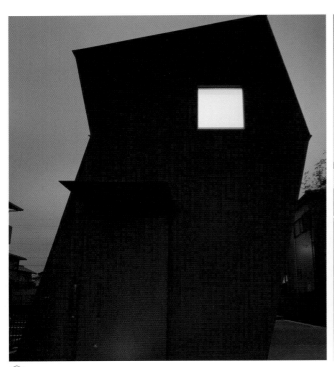 

View of the Refraction House at night: the window lights up, like an eye peering out to keep watch.

Vue de la maison Réfraction House » la nuit : la fenêtre s'illumine, à l'instar d'un œil qui surveille.

Das Refraktionshaus in der Nacht: das erhellte Fenster sieht aus wie ein Auge, das Wache hält.

e bathroom surface is made of concrete while the floors feature ceramic tiles, emphasizing the simplicity and strength on which this residence is built.

surface de la salle de bains est en béton et les sols sont en carreaux de céramique, soulignant la simplicité et la sobriété de la construction.

e Badezimmerflächen sind aus Beton und die Böden gefliest, ein Zeichen für das einfache, strenge Design des Hauses.

Vacation Home in Furx
Maison de vacances à Furx
Ferienhaus in Furx

Marte.Marte Architekten

What at first sight seems to be a closed, modest structure, very similar to the neighboring houses in this Austrian province, is really an exercise in design, the principal theme of which is the arrangement of the exterior openings. Since the plot is located on a mountain top, the designers took advantage of the views while integrating the building with the architecture typical of small houses in the region. The house's four main glass surfaces produce four sets of images; the architects describe them as four lenses with different exposure mechanisms. Inside this plain, austere unit, the layout is based on a cross, with four spaces that are open and connected to each other. Each room has a closed surface and a window that creates an effect of depth from both inside and outside, as the position of the pane can be changed. This effect, repeated on all four sides, gives the building a solid, magical appearance.

Ce qui, à première vue, semble être une structure fermée et modeste, identique aux maisons environnantes de cette province d'Autriche, est en réalité un exercice de design axé sur l'agencement des ouvertures extérieures. Le terrain situé au sommet de la montagne a permis aux designers de jouer sur les vues tout en intégrant la construction à l'architecture typique des petites maisons de la région. A l'instar de quatre séries d'images, les quatre principales surfaces de verre de la maison sont conçues par les architectes comme quatre lentilles d'objectif, réglées sur différents temps d'expositions. A l'intérieur de cette unité austère et pure, le tracé cruciforme est doté de quatre espaces ouverts qui communiquent entre eux. Chaque pièce a une surface fermée et une fenêtre créant un effet de profondeur à l'intérieur comme à l'extérieur, grâce à la position modulable du carreau. Cet effet, répété sur les quatre côtés, accentue l'aspect magique de l'édifice.

Was zunächst wie eine geschlossene, eher bescheidene Struktur im Stil der Nachbarhäuser dieser österreichischen Provinz anmutet, ist tatsächlich ein meisterlicher Entwurf, dessen Hauptthema das Zusammenspiel der Verbindungen nach außen ist. Da das Grundstück direkt auf einem Bergrücken steht, haben die Architekten den Blick auf die herrliche Landschaft in die Gestaltung des Hauses mit einbezogen. Die vier großen Fenster des Hauses bieten einen Ausblick auf vier verschiedene Landschaftsbilder, die Architekten beschreiben diese als vier Linsen mit unterschiedlichen Belichtungsmechanismen. Innerhalb dieser einfachen, eher streng ausgelegten Struktur ist das Gebäude in eine Kreuzform mit vier untereinander verbundenen Flächen unterteilt. Jedes Zimmer ist in sich geschlossen und hat ein Fenster. Die Position der Fensterscheiben kann geändert werden. Das verleiht dem Gebäude ein solides, fast magisches Aussehen.

Plan Plan Grundriss

Ground floor Rez-de-chaussée Erdgeschoss

First floor Premier étage Erstes Obergeschoss

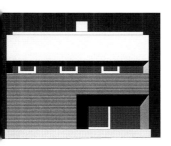

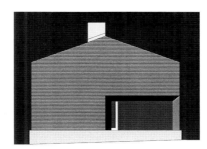

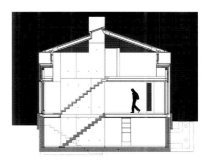

Section Section Schnitt

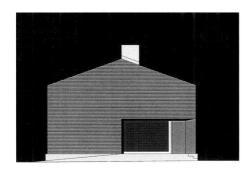

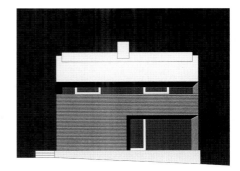

Elevations Élévations Aufrisse

The house's monolithic appearance solves the problems related to its placement while blending with the austere look of the neighboring structures.

L'aspect monolithique de la maison résout la question de son emplacement, en l'assimilant aux structures environnantes.

Das monolithische Erscheinungsbild des Hauses passt perfekt zu dem Standort und dem nüchternen Stil der Umgebung.

The house, for the most part a structure made of prefabricated elements, is supported on a concrete base that serves as a foundation but keeps it off the ground.

La maison, une structure en grande partie faite d'éléments préfabriqués, repose sur un socle de béton qui, à l'instar de fondations, la surélève du sol.

Das Haus besteht überwiegend aus vorgefertigten Elementen und steht auf einem Betonfundament, das gleichzeitig Empore ist.

h room has a closed surface and a window that creates an effect of depth from both inside and outside.

aque pièce est dotée d'une surface fermée et d'une fenêtre créant un effet de profondeur à l'intérieur comme à l'extérieur.

Räume sind von geschlossenen Flächen mit je einem Fenster umgeben, wodurch ein Effekt der Tiefe erzeugt wird.

☐ Levis House
Maison Levis
Levis Haus

UdA and Davide Volpe

On the site of a small, old hayloft, Studio UdA put up a two-story building whose composition was conceived as a filter between landscape and architecture. The client requested that several spaces be treated as extensions to the functions of the existing building. Both floors were fitted with an outdoor staircase and linked to the farmstead. The interior layout was straightforward: the ground floor, kitchen, bathroom and living room on the first floor, and the dining room and terrace on the second. As the building is surrounded by an orchard and situated on the edge of a slope facing the Alps, the new rooms were envisioned as filters that gradually lead from the enclosed interior spaces of the original building to the boundary between the structure and the vast stretch of land. Both sides of the house rest on a bed of small stones, while the main façade opens onto a landscaped garden of trees and small shrubs.

Sur le site d'un ancien petit fenil, le Studio UdA a construit un édifice de deux étages, conçu à l'instar d'un filtre entre le paysage et l'architecture. A la demande du client, plusieurs espaces ont été conçus comme le prolongement fonctionnel du bâtiment déjà existant. Les deux étages dotés d'un escalier extérieur sont reliés à la ferme. La conception de l'intérieur est simple : rez-de-chaussée, cuisine, salle de bains et salon au premier étage, la salle à manger et la terrasse au deuxième. Entourées d'un verger et situées en haut d'une colline face aux Alpes, les nouvelles pièces du bâtiment ont été conçues à l'image d'un filtre passant graduellement des espaces intérieurs fermés de l'édifice initial vers les espaces qui délimitent la structure et la vaste étendue de terre. Les deux côtés de la maison reposent sur un lit de petites pierres tandis que la façade principale s'ouvre sur jardin paysager, orné d'arbres et de petits buissons.

Auf einem ehemaligen kleinen, alten Heuschober hat Studio UdA ein zweigeschossiges Gebäude errichtet. Der Kunde hatte darum gebeten, dass verschiedene Räume als Erweiterung der Funktion des bestehenden Gebäudes genutzt würden. Beide Etagen wurden mit einer Außentreppe versehen und mit dem Bauernhaus verbunden. Die Innenausstattung ist ausgesprochen klar und eindeutig: Erdgeschoss, Küche Badezimmer und Wohnzimmer im ersten Stock und Esszimmer und Terrasse im zweiten. Das Gebäude ist von einer alten Obstplantage umgeben und liegt direkt am Rande einer Skipiste liegt die auf die Alpen weist. Daher wurden die neuen Räume quasi als Filter konzipiert, bei dem die Grenze zwischen den geschlossenen inneren Räumen des ursprünglichen Gebäudes und der kargen Natur aufgelöst werden soll. Beide Seiten des Hauses ruhen auf einem Fundament aus kleinen Steinen, während die Hauptfassade auf einen gepflegten Garten mit Bäumen und kleineren Büschen weist.

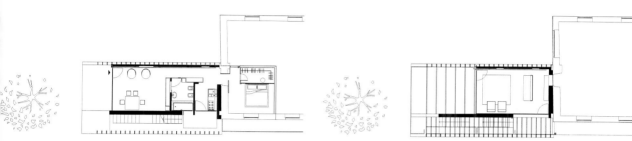

round floor Rez-de-chaussée Erdgeschoss

First floor Premier étage Erstes Obergeschoss

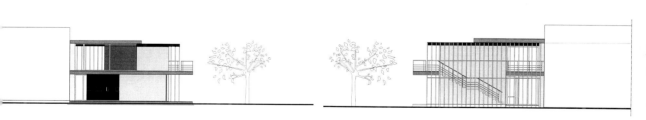

ngitudinal section Section longitudinale Längsschnitt

Section Section Schnitt

This house, annexed to a pre-existing rural building, is sheltered by a laminated wood structure and surrounded by a beautifully landscaped garden.

Cette maison, annexée à une construction rurale préexistante est protégée par une structure en bois laminé et entourée d'un jardin magnifiquement bien agencé.

Dieser Anbau zu einem ländlichen Haus wird durch eine Holzstruktur geschützt. Ringsherum liegt ein wunderschöner Garten.

The entrance façade incorporates a glass wall that exposes the minimalist dining area as well as an upper terrace adjoining the bedroom.

Un mur de verre, incorporé à la façade principale, expose la salle à manger minimaliste ainsi que la terrasse supérieure adjacente à la pièce.

Durch die Glaswand an der Vorderfront sieht man den minimalistischen Essbereich. Oben die an das Schlafzimmer angrenzende Terrasse.

Coelho house
Maison Coelho
Coelho Haus

Andrade & Morettin

This house consists of two interconnected volumes arranged along a longitudinal axis. The main body is a foyer, consisting of a jatobá timber framework surrounded by light, polycarbonate panels. This translucent membrane gives way at one of its corners to the transparency of glass, framing the view over a nearby lake. A curtain that occasionally defines a dark, more private environment establishes the limits of the bedroom area. For both formal and constructional reasons, this light box stands above the ground on a support, while the floating corrugated, sheet-metal roof contributes to the effect of weightlessness. The service area, containing the kitchen, washroom, bathroom and gas tanks, is conceived as a rock that emerges from the ground in the form of wide ceramic walls, thus protecting the main pavilion from the rays of the afternoon sun.

Cette maison comporte deux volumes reliés entre eux le long d'un axe longitudinal. Le foyer est le corps principal, formé d'une charpente en bois de jatoba entourée de panneaux légers en poly carbonate. Dans un de ses angles, cette membrane translucide cède la place à la transparence du verre qui encadre la vue au-dessus d'un lac situé à proximité. Un rideau sert de séparation occasionnelle à un espace sombre et plus privé, la sphère de la chambre à coucher. Pour des raisons à la fois de forme et de construction, cette boite légère, surplombe le sol grâce à un support et le toit flottant en feuille de métal ondulé, souligne l'effet de légèreté. La zone de services comportant la cuisine, la laverie, la salle de bains et la cuve à gaz, est conçue comme un rocher émergeant du sol sous la forme de murs blancs en céramique, protégeant ainsi le pavillon des rayons du soleil de l'après-midi.

Dieses Haus besteht aus zwei miteinander verbundenen Einheiten, die in einer Längsachse ausgerichtet sind. Den Hauptbereich bildet ein Foyer, das aus Jatoba-Holz gerahmt wurde und mit leichten Paneelen aus Polycarbonat umgeben ist. Diese durchscheinende Membran wird an einer Ecke durch ein Glasfenster durchbrochen, das den Rahmen für einen herrlichen Ausblick auf den nahe gelegenen See bietet. Ein Vorhang, mit dem der Raum auch abgedunkelt werden kann, bildet die Grenze zum Schlafbereich. Sowohl aus formellen, aber auch aus bautechnischen Gründen steht diese leichte Kiste auf einer Stützstruktur, während das fließende, Wellblechdach den Eindruck von Schwerelosigkeit noch verstärkt. Der Nutzbereich mit Küche, Waschraum, Badezimmer und Gastanks wird als Felsen empfunden, der in Form von breiten Keramikwänden aus dem Boden wächst und so den Hauptpavillon vor den Strahlen der Nachmittagssonne schützt.

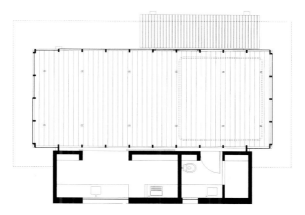

Plan Plan Grundriss

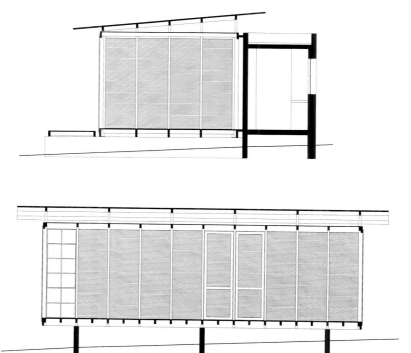

Sections Sections Schnitte

The distorted perception of the polycarbonate panels places the house somewhere between abstraction and reality.

La perception déformée des panneaux de poly carbonate inscrit la maison entre abstraction et réalité.

Die verzerrte Wahrnehmung der Tafeln aus Polykarbonat lässt das Haus wie eine Mischung aus Abstraktion und Realität wirken.

The various possible readings of this architectural object are evoked by the different degrees of transparency of its skin.

Les diverses possibilités de lecture de cette œuvre architecturale sont dues aux différents degrés de transparence de son revêtement.

Die verschiedenen Lesarten dieses Projekts werden durch die unterschiedlichen Transparenzgrade der Gebäudehaut hervorgerufen.

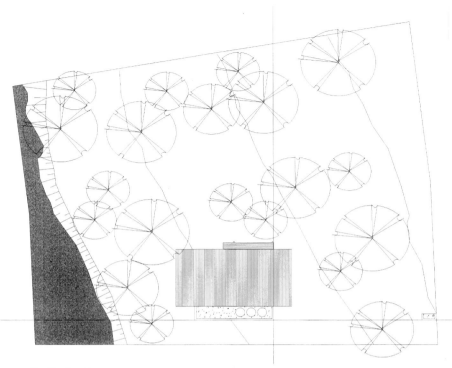

Plan Plan Grundriss

☐ Ithaca House
Maison Ithaca
Haus in Ithaca

Simon Ungers

The conceptual starting point for this project was the desire to create a monolithic, sculpture-like structure in the midst of this vast, upstate New York landscape. To take the best advantage of the views of a nearby ravine and the woods that cover a third of the property, the house was situated at the edge of the lot. The home, used as a getaway for short periods or on weekends, is divided into two levels. On the ground floor of this cube-like structure there is a parking area and a small office, while the upper floor houses the kitchen, bathroom, living room, and bedroom, separated from the rest of the space by low shelves. The exterior consists of concrete blocks with a minimum of joints, emphasizing the building's sturdy, solid structure. The roof is used as an outdoor terrace. From here, one can enjoy splendid views of the valley, the woods, and the ravine and still be shielded from the untamed surroundings.

L'architecte a eu l'idée de créer une habitation dotée d'une structure compacte de panneaux d'aluminium, munis d'ouvertures extérieures réglées par un système de contrôle précis, dans un souci d'harmonie entre la maison et le dock d'un canal navigable. Deux grandes ouvertures au nord et à l'est brisent le caisson en métal créant ainsi une sensation d'espace. A l'intérieur, le choix des matériaux légers engendre un espace très chaleureux. Le sol de la cuisine est recouvert de panneaux de béton rouge foncé, couleur qui se retrouve dans les meubles de cuisine et dans la zone centrale, avec la cheminée. Dans la partie ouest de la maison, la salle de bains et les chambres alignées débouchent sur un couloir. Plutôt que d'être concentrés en un point, les corridors traversent tout l'espace. Par simple pression sur un bouton, un escalier escamotable en acier permet d'accéder à un petit loft, ce qui n'est pas sans rappeler l'aspect nautique de l'ensemble.

Konzeptuell war eine monolithische, skulpturähnliche Struktur inmitten der kargen Landschaft von Upstate New York geplant. Um die Aussicht auf eine nahe gelegene Schlucht und die umgebenden Wälder so weit es geht mit einzubeziehen, wurde das Haus an den Rand des Grundstückes verlegt. Das Gebäude selber wird hauptsächlich für kurze Wochenendausflüge genutzt und ist in zwei Ebenen unterteilt. Im Erdgeschoss dieser Kubusähnlichen Struktur befinden sich eine Garage und ein kleines Büro. Im Obergeschoss befinden sich die Küche, das Badezimmer, das Wohn- und das Schlafzimmer, das von den anderen Zimmern durch niedrige Regale abgetrennt wurde. Außen ist das Gebäude mit Betonplatten verkleidet, die zu der robusten, soliden Struktur des Hauses beitragen. Das Dach wird als Terrasse genutzt. Von hier aus genießt man einen wunderschönen Blick auf das Tal, die Bäume und die Schlucht und bleibt doch gleichzeitig abgeschirmt von der umgebenden Landschaft.

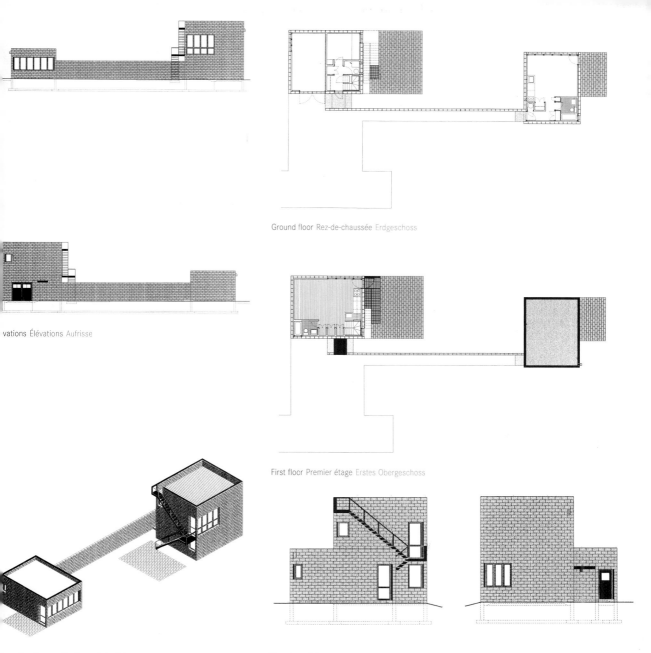

Ground floor Rez-de-chaussée Erdgeschoss

vations Élévations Aufrisse

First floor Premier étage Erstes Obergeschoss

spective Perspective Perspektivzeichnung

Elevations Élévations Aufrisse

The building was conceived as a basic, solid, uniform shape with the aim of creating a small residence in which the vast landscape plays a dominant role.

Le concept de base de cette construction repose sur une forme simple, compacte et uniforme, pour créer une petite résidence où l'immense paysage environnant joue un grand rôle.

Das kleine Wohnhaus wurde als solides, gleichmäßiges Gebäude angelegt, das von der weiten Landschaft ringsherum dominiert wird.

⌂ A narrow, metal outer staircase, standing out from the mass of the house, connects the ground floor patio with the living area and roof terrace.

Un escalier extérieur, étroit, se détachant de la masse de la maison, relie le patio du rez-de-chaussée au salon et à la terrasse de toit.

Eine schmale Außentreppe verbindet den Patio im Erdgeschoss mit dem Wohnbereich und der Dachterrasse.

]
ide and out, the materials reinforce the idea of a small refuge and monolithic sculpture.

'intérieur comme à l'extérieur, les matériaux exaltent le double concept de petit refuge et de sculpture monolithique.

e innen und außen verwendeten Materialien lassen das Haus wie eine monolithische Plastik wirken.

e minimalist approach to details and finishes fully reflects the basic character of the home.

pproche minimaliste des détails et de la finition reflète parfaitement le caractère de la maison.

r minimalistische Ansatz bei Details und Oberflächen spiegelt den einfachen Charakter des Hauses wieder.

☐ Cozy Cabin
Cabane confortable
Gemütliche Hütte

Wingårdh Arkitektkontor

This small villa, located in a small town and surrounded by a charming setting of abundant trees and fallen leaves, was previously a mill that formed part of a farm. The house is divided into two levels, and takes advantage of the high, pitched roof to insert a bedroom into a mezzanine. The communal area downstairs includes the living room, kitchen, bathroom, and sauna. A concealed stairway leads to the distinctive bedroom, which has two triangular walls beneath steeply sloping ceilings. Everything, except the glass and concrete fireplace and the stone floor downstairs, is lined with a light, natural wood. In certain areas, the wood has been given a different grain by using smaller planks to set these spaces off from the main supporting walls. From the outside, the house has the appeal of an inviting, warm cabin, while its doors open out onto Sweden´s picturesque countryside.

Cette petite villa, située dans une petite ville au cœur d'un charmant paysage boisé, tapissé de feuilles mortes, est en fait un ancien moulin de ferme. La maison, à deux niveaux, tire parti de la hauteur du toit pour y intégrer une chambre à coucher sur mezzanine. En bas, les parties communes comprennent le salon, la cuisine, la salle de bain et le sauna. Un escalier dissimulé conduit à une chambre spéciale, dotée de deux murs triangulaires coiffés d'un toit haut et pentu. L'ensemble, à l'exception de la cheminée en verre et béton et de l'escalier en pierre, est revêtu de boiseries naturelles et claires. A certains endroits, la texture du bois est diversifiée par l'ajout de plus petites lattes faisant ressortir ces espaces des principaux murs porteurs. Avec le charme extérieur d'une cabane accueillante et confortable, cette maison vous invite à en ouvrir les portes qui donnent sur la pittoresque campagne suédoise.

Diese kleine Villa, die in einem kleinen Dorf errichtet wurde liegt inmitten eines dichten Waldes und diente früher als Mühle. Das Haus ist in zwei Ebenen unterteilt und in dem hoch aufgeschlagenen Dach wurde in einem Zwischengeschoss noch ein Schlafzimmer untergebracht. Im gemeinsamen Wohnbereich unten wurden Wohnzimmer, Küche, Badezimmer und eine Sauna eingerichtet. Ein verputztes Treppenhaus führt zum Schlafzimmer, das aus zwei dreieckigen Wänden unter steil abfallenden Decken besteht. Alle Innenwände außer dem Kamin aus Glas und Beton, sowie den Steinböden im Erdgeschoss, wurden mit hellem, natürlichem Holz verkleidet. In bestimmten Bereichen wurde dem Holz eine andere Ausrichtung gegeben indem schmalere Bretter eingesetzt wurden, um diese Bereiche von den Hauptstützwänden abzutrennen. Von außen sieht man in eine einladende, gemütliche Hütte hinein, die Türöffnungen bieten einen herrlichen Ausblick auf die malerische Landschaft Schwedens.

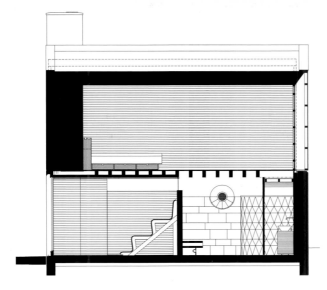

Section Section Schnitt

] From the exterior, the house has the look of an invitingly warm cabin. Its doors open on to a platform standing over the waters of the nearby stream.

De l'extérieur, la maison a des allures de cabane chaleureuse et accueillante. Ses portes s'ouvrent sur une plate-forme qui surplombe les eaux de la rivière voisine.

Schon von Außen sieht das Haus sehr behaglich aus. Die Türen führen zu einer Plattform über dem nahen Fluss.

In certain areas, the wood has been given a different grain by using smaller planks, thereby contrasting these sections with the main supporting walls.

A certains endroits, le bois prend une nouvelle texture grâce à l'apport de lattes plus petites, pour créer un contraste entre ces parties et les principaux murs porteurs.

An einigen Stellen hat das Holz durch die Verwendung kleinerer Planken eine andere Maserung, was im Kontrast zu den Wänden steht.

The overwhelming presence of wood in the bedroom requires little else in the way of decoration: a comfortable bed, a shelf, and intimate lighting are enough to give the room a welcoming feel.

L'omniprésence du bois dans la chambre à coucher simplifie le décor : un lit confortable, une étagère et un éclairage intime suffisent à rendre la pièce accueillante.

Die allgegenwärtige Präsenz von Holz im Schlafzimmer macht eine Dekoration neben Bett, Regal und warmer Beleuchtung überflüssig.

Photo credits Crédits photographiques Fotonachweis